MELANIE PUMP

DETOX

Managing

INSECURITY

in the

WORKPLACE

LIONCREST
PUBLISHING

For all my friends and family,

who have been with me through the most difficult

times and the very best times as well.

I've learned from you and have become

who I am today through you.

CONTENTS

ACKNOWLEDGMENTS

Thank you to all those who helped me through their ideas and support to write this book. Special thanks to Mike Watson, Mona Forster, Kim Deschaine, Sarah Pump, Liz Chang, and last but not least, my mother, Susan Ross.

MY STORY

It would be fair to question why a financial executive would write a book about the impact of insecurity in the workplace. Books about the mental well-being of employees are typically written by human resource professionals or psychologists, not by people in my field.

However, my life's journey has made me an expert in insecurity, its effects, and how to mitigate them. And my work experiences have shown me the impact that leaders and work environments have on the level of insecurity that employees feel.

Twenty years in the corporate world have led me to my current role as chief financial officer (CFO) for a technology company. Prior to this, I held other high-level corporate positions, including CFO in a large international software conglomerate, and vice-president of finance in a North American e-commerce company. However, my trajectory to the C-suite didn't follow the standard route. This is what sets me apart from many of my peers.

My early years were marred by family drama. Not long after I was born, my family lost all of its assets to bankruptcy, and we were forced to leave our home. My parents' marriage was already unstable and was unable to recover from this shock. They divorced.

The family crises continued throughout my childhood. By my fifteenth birthday, I had left my family home and escaped into drugs. I spent many nights sleeping on the streets. It's hard to imagine a more insecure situation: alone, not knowing where I would even sleep each night or what my future would bring.

My insecurities made the high school environment unmanageable for me, and I dropped out before completing grade ten.

However, my natural resilience and intelligence eventually awakened and won out, and when I was eighteen, I committed to quitting drugs and building a new life.

After a few years working in hospitality, I landed my first corporate job as a receptionist at an engineering firm. Although I wasn't aware of the ultimate destination at that time, this was the start of my path to becoming a CFO.

My purpose in sharing this story is not to gain your sympathy but to paint a picture of the challenges that an employee can overcome with the right support in a healthy work environment.

Given my life experiences to that point, I felt profoundly different from my peers and insecure about it. I was fortunate that my first corporate environment was healthy and had supportive leaders. I didn't realize my potential, but those leaders saw the potential in me, even though I didn't. They supported me to attend night school toward my bachelor's degree. With their encouragement, I began to believe in myself and to overcome my insecurities.

I would later learn that healthy, supportive work environments are not the norm in the corporate world. Since that first job, I've been in as many toxic work environments as I have healthy ones. I've seen the harmful behaviors that toxic workplaces bring out in employees. These behaviors are people's efforts to protect themselves, but they often work against the success of both the employees and the business.

The dichotomy between healthy workplaces and toxic ones is my trigger for this book.

Although my early work experiences showed me the power of a supportive corporate culture, I became certain of the difficulty to heal and grow in toxic work environments when I went through another challenging period later in my life.

My life partner unexpectedly died before the age of forty. Unfortunately, my workplaces during this time of grief were toxic. The negativity in those environments made it even harder for me to manage my anguish and mental health. It felt impossible to heal while surrounded by negativity every day.

To protect me, my subconscious pushed for the use of defensive behaviors, which I will discuss in this book. I had to manage these impulses while in leadership roles responsible for business objectives and the success of others.

When I felt a corporate culture was too detrimental to my mental health, I chose a better life for myself and resigned. I've been empowered to do this because I know better environments exist. But how many people are struggling in toxic workplaces because they don't believe there's a better option? I believe this number is high.

A toxic work environment is not damaging to employees alone. I passionately believe that as it stands, many corporate leaders are doing a disservice to employees, businesses, *and* investors by tolerating harmful conduct in the workplace and accepting unhealthy work environments.

My heart and values influence my theories, but as a finance professional, I will also tell you that toxic corporate cultures hurt the bottom line: we are wasting resources when we accept them. The high levels of insecurity triggered in these environments limit employees' ability to perform at their full potential. We are risking underperformance and missed objectives when we don't actively promote healthy, supportive workplaces.

Even companies that appear to be doing well (and I have worked at some of them) could be performing better if harmful workplace behaviors and approaches that create insecurity were no longer accepted.

■　■　■

This book is written for current and future leaders who are open to thinking differently and making positive change in the corporate world.

It will first lay out the core elements of human nature and brain function that are the foundation for workplace security and insecurity. Next, it explores and describes the factors in the workplace that trigger and magnify insecurities and the steps that leaders can take to mitigate these factors and create a corporate culture that will enable employees to produce their best work.

The observations and insights conveyed here will also be valuable to anyone seeking to learn what drives us from deep within. I will tell stories that are based on real experiences. The names and details have been carefully changed to maintain anonymity; however, the emotional tone of the situations and the impact on the people in them are real.

You may recognize yourself and others in the stories that I describe. The negative behaviors portrayed in the stories are often not who we really are; they are reactions to our situations, and they don't have to happen. Often, it's self-preservation instincts driven by threats that causes undesirable conduct. Remove the danger in the environment and the harmful behavior will reduce, too.

■   ■   ■

Before we move on, I want to note that although I am discussing aspects of mental health, I'm not an expert on mental illness. What I'm sharing in this book are my observations and learnings from my twenty years in both healthy and toxic work environments. My research is my study of the natural but impactful human reactions that I have seen in these environments.

Mental illnesses are significant factors in the workplace but should be addressed by trained psychologists and medical professionals. If the behavior of an employee or leader appears to deviate to the level of mental illness, it should be taken seriously and when possible, in consideration of privacy, professional assistance should be recommended.

CHAPTER 1

THE REALITY OF INSECURITY: WE ALL HAVE IT

Throughout my life, I've had times of deep insecurity. There have been times when I didn't have shelter or enough money for good food; times when I felt like an impostor in my field and times when I felt threatened by a bullying boss.

All of us have been through challenging periods like these. We've all had experiences that have created insecurities about some aspect of our self or our life. Although some of us deny feeling it, insecurity is a common emotion.

WHAT IS INSECURITY?

Before we go on, let's get on the same page and create a common understanding of the word *insecurity*.

My definition of insecurity is a feeling of danger or vulnerability —a feeling that our mental or physical state is at risk. This feeling may be rooted in a lack of confidence in our abilities, uncertainty about our future, or the perception of threats in our environment.

When insecurity is at a high level, it can increase feelings of self-doubt and anxiety. We may start to question whether we can handle the challenges of life. Sometimes even mundane tasks can seem too hard. We have a lower tolerance for uncertainty, risk, or stress and an increased drive to protect ourselves against these factors.

Insecurity is usually judged in our culture to be a weakness; the word *insecure* is even used as an insult. This creates a pressure to hide our insecurities because we're scared that exposing them will limit our opportunities.

The reality is that feeling insecure is natural and even necessary. The feeling activates an instinct that drives us toward security and pushes us away from danger and toxicity. We may be conscious of our need for security, but I've found it's more often a pursuit driven by our subconscious mind. Our active mind is not always truly aware that our instinct for security is what's causing us to act in certain ways or make certain decisions. Our need for security is *that* primal.

This primal need can lead to positive effects. It can be harnessed to drive healthy change. Some people even channel their insecurity to drive them toward success. Barbara Corcoran, a real estate mogul and *Shark Tank* expert, admitted that insecurities from her childhood were one of her drivers (Connor 2013):

*"It's so hard to shake those things you
carry with you from your childhood and past.
But if you have something like that inside of you, wrap
your arms around it and make it your friend.
Find a way to use it. Insecurity makes
you run. What's wrong with that?"*

Barbara Corcoran's success is an above-average example, but for all of us, our efforts to increase our sense of security can help us shape and build our lives. Getting an education, finding a life partner, and choosing a career are often driven by the pursuit of security. My decisions to get a corporate job and go back to school were driven by this pursuit. They were powerful choices that turned my life around.

However, feelings of insecurity can also have negative effects. When our sense of insecurity is at a high level, it can push us to do things that aren't good for us. If the danger feels immediate, we may take short-term actions that don't benefit our long-term goals.

Case in point: I resigned from a position even though I didn't have a new job yet because my work environment felt dangerously toxic. A bullying boss had been seriously affecting my mental health and I'd become very insecure. Unarguably, resigning was an extremely risky short-term action because it's harder to find a job when you don't already have one. Nevertheless, my psyche told me that the immediate dangers of staying in that workplace were too severe. I pushed long-term career and financial goals aside for the short-term goal of protecting my mental health.

Was this the right decision? It's hard to know for sure: even though I did remove myself from a psychologically unsafe environment, there may have been another alternative that I was blind to in my singular focus to escape the danger of my bullying boss.

Ironically, insecurity can manifest in a different form, one that has an opposite negative effect: the fear of uncertainty or change. When we experience that form of insecurity, our fears lock us into remaining in situations that are harmful or that limit our personal and professional growth. We can be too scared to take even the small risks that are required to move forward in life.

Until I overcame my insecurities, I stayed in my safe accounting field and didn't share my story. I was too scared to put myself out into the world. This was a subconscious decision to protect myself that limited my growth and my ability to contribute.

I think many of us are letting fear and insecurity drive unproductive behaviors and actions or hold us back. Our growth and contributions are limited, and if the drive is at a subconscious level, we may not even realize it.

THE PREVALENCE OF INSECURITY IN OUR SOCIETY

Feeling insecure is certainly not a novel human experience, but I think the prevalence of people with debilitating levels of insecurity is on the rise today. Many factors impact our sense of security. Common situations in adult life, such as career or relationship problems, can make us feel insecure. Aspects of our childhoods also may have created insecurities.

My early experiences certainly created them, and they've challenged me all through my adult life. And I'm not alone in this. These deep-rooted insecurities can be triggered by current-day situations, re-creating the same self-doubt and fears from earlier in our lives.

However, significant new factors in today's modern world are contributing to our insecurities as well: higher levels of divorce, political and philosophical divides, and climate change all put a huge strain on us.

Compounding this is a web of social media that makes it difficult to escape the negativity. It also provides an easily accessible platform to compare ourselves to others. A tour through any social media app will show us someone who appears to be doing better, looking better, and living better than we are. Even though I've exceeded my own expectations (and have done well by societal standards), I can still feel my insecurity rise as I scroll through LinkedIn or Instagram. These apps constantly present us with the "glossy" versions that people choose to show of themselves. It would be difficult for anyone not to feel their security waver when faced with those images.

All of these factors are combining to increase the level of insecurity we feel today. My belief is that each of us has a limited capacity for how much insecurity we can handle. We can take only so many hits to our psyche before our maximum threshold is reached. When our proverbial bucket is full of insecurity, that is when it can drive protective behaviors. Because these protective instincts can negatively impact our lives, and, in turn, our behavior, a higher prevalence of general insecurity will increase the risk of toxicity in all the environments we enter, including our work environments.

INSECURITY AT WORK

Given the many hours we spend at work, our experiences there significantly contribute to our sense of well-being. The work environment can have a positive influence by building our confidence, equipping us to counter any insecurity created in other parts of our lives. However, it can also undermine our sense of security.

If issues at work have us brimming over with self-doubt, we may exceed our capacity to manage our insecurity. Likewise, if our work environment is toxic, that will greatly reduce our feelings of security.

I've used the word *toxic* to describe a work environment many times already, but I'll clarify what I mean by that. This clarity is important since toxic work environments are a common trigger for insecurity and will be discussed a lot throughout this book.

Our perception of threats to our mental state from within a toxic work environment can lead to feelings of anxiety and insecurity. The threats may come from toxic behaviors used by those within the environments. Sometimes just a person's negativity can put us in a bad mood; however, the conduct can be overt and affect us more seriously as well. Toxic behavior includes bullying, harassment, and lying.

If we sense a threat that we could be psychologically harmed by a person, environment, or situation, we will put up defenses, often unconsciously, to protect ourselves. These defenses, unfortunately, can themselves be toxic, such as avoidance or passive-aggressive behavior.

In fact, this is how the work environment itself often becomes toxic. The toxicity may begin from only one employee's conduct, but the toxicity spreads throughout the workplace due to the protective behaviors that initial employee's conduct elicits from others. Everyone in the environment will sense the threats and feelings of insecurity will increase.

However, toxic behaviors aren't the only causes of toxicity in a workplace. As you will learn later in the book, aspects of someone's job or employer can negatively impact their sense of security if there's significant uncertainty around the safety of their position, a lack of transparency around their company's direction, or if the employee is in a role that they aren't right or ready for.

This book will lay out the reality that when a work environment is toxic and drives up employees' insecurities, it impacts their performance and reduces an organization's ability to meet its objectives.

Yet, the impact of insecurity isn't directly discussed in business courses, and it has never been a topic at any boardroom table I've sat at, with one exception: when an employee was being talked about critically. At those times, no one asked *why* the person was insecure or *what* in the environment might be creating or magnifying their insecurity, much less what the company could do to reduce its causes.

That is why this book is necessary. Leaders need to accept the reality of insecurity and be thoughtful about reducing it. We need to stop accepting toxic environments that, at best, maintain employees' insecurities at a tolerable level or, at worst, magnify them. We need to do this for our teams and for the business owners and investors we're responsible to.

And we need to do it for *ourselves*. As leaders, we need a psychologically healthy work environment, too; just because we've achieved a position of authority, that doesn't mean that we don't have our own insecurities.

However, as leaders, we have a greater ability to enact the changes needed to create healthy workplaces. And because the behavior of leaders sets the bar for acceptable employee conduct, we have a great responsibility not to display the toxic behaviors I will describe. We have the duty and the power to make a positive difference.

Now that we've established the reality of insecurity, we can move on to how security factors into our human needs, the defenses that we use to ensure those needs are met, and the power of the subconscious.

CHAPTER 2

THE DRIVE FOR SECURITY

The impact of the subconscious mind is mentioned often throughout this book. I believe that our subconscious has significant power over our behaviors, more than many of us realize. This power is particularly strong when we're in an insecure mental state. At those times, our subconscious takes charge in an attempt to defend us and ensure that our needs are met. The pursuit of these needs and the use of these defenses can be intentional, but, in my experience, they're often driven by our subconscious.

This chapter introduces a needs theory and outlines common defense mechanisms we use to protect ourselves.

MASLOW'S HIERARCHY OF NEEDS

I was first introduced to the power of unmet needs when I was thirty. My counselor was trying to help me understand why I was in crisis.

After working hard to turn my life around, I no longer had to add up the price of my groceries while I shopped. I had a great job in a healthy work environment, and I was in a stable, loving relationship, yet I felt like something was still missing. This is when I was introduced to Maslow's hierarchy of needs.

The hierarchy of needs was developed in 1943 by psychologist Abraham Maslow. A scientific theory of human behavior, it suggests that human beings are motivated to fulfill basic needs before focusing on the fulfillment of complex needs. The chart below outlines these needs.

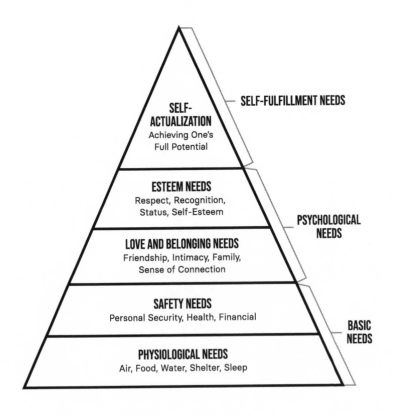

In my early years, all of my focus had to be on fulfilling the base level, physiological needs (food, water, shelter, etc.). By the point in my life when I entered therapy, I was readily able to fulfill those needs, and my needs for safety and love were also met. I was craving the fulfillment of needs I'd never thought about before: achieving self-esteem and reaching my full potential.

As a woman who hadn't even graduated from grade ten, I had never thought about my "full potential." But now that I had exceeded all my modest expectations, I was learning that what was keeping me up at night was my inner need to reach that potential.

Maslow's theory turned a light on for me, and I've seen it play out in my life and the lives of others ever since.

How does the hierarchy of needs relate to insecurity? The second tier, safety needs—in my terminology, our need for security—is the focus of this book. Safety needs encompass both physical and mental health. It is my belief that if our "insecurity bucket" is overflowing, we have an unmet need for mental safety.

In that state, our psyche perceives our mental health to be at risk, so it becomes hyperfocused on reducing that risk. As a result, we will have a difficult time concentrating on our work unless the work objective helps us fulfill that need.

In some cases, our actions to meet our need for safety can even work against achieving high performance in our roles. For example, we may get defensive when given constructive feedback because it's too mentally threatening, but this stops us from hearing input that could help us improve.

Until we feel safe, we will also be less influenced by the potential benefits of fulfilling higher-level needs. This should be a significant concern for employers since many of the tactics business's use to motivate their workforces are aligned with the higher-level needs in Maslow's hierarchy: recognition, belonging, and self-actualization.

An employee's ability to even consider those higher-level needs will reduce as their insecurity deepens. The immediate drive to seek safety will cloud comparably minor desires. We will not be as focused on the potential of promotions or meeting objectives if we're busy trying to protect our mental health.

My personal experience has supported this theory. When I was in toxic workplaces, I couldn't work to my full potential or be the strong leader that I know I'm capable of being. I was too concerned with my own mental health. I also became much less concerned with esteem. I willingly left high-profile jobs because I felt that my mental health was significantly at risk due to the toxicity of the work environment.

There has been criticism of Maslow's theory which mainly states that the needs may not follow the hierarchical order that Maslow has laid out and that there's little evidence to support a hierarchy (Wahba and Bridwell 1976). For example, even if our safety needs aren't fully met, we may still have a need for loving relationships and feelings of belonging.

I think this criticism is fair, and I don't believe that we're completely incapable of thinking about the higher-level needs until the lower-level needs are fulfilled. However, I do believe that focus will be reduced. We won't be able to achieve our full potential if an unfulfilled lower-level need distracts us. I think this is particularly true with the need for safety.

If our mental or physical safety is threatened, we will find it very difficult to focus elsewhere. The distraction will intensify as the level of danger does. I think you will agree this is indisputable for physical safety, and I argue that it's the same for mental safety. When our mental state is threatened, I believe we will defend it as we do our physical state.

Maslow's hierarchy isn't bulletproof, but it does offer a helpful perspective. It's a tool that, like it did for me, may help you understand what drives and motivates your employees (and yourself).

DEFENSE MECHANISMS

*"Without comedy as a defense mechanism,
I wouldn't be able to survive."*

—GARRY SHANDLING

Garry Shandling's defense mechanisms worked very well for him as a stand-up comedian and actor. Unfortunately, not all of us are as able to turn our defense mechanisms into a long, lucrative career.

Defense mechanisms are mental tools that we unconsciously use to protect ourselves from psychological threats. These threats could be presented by situations or thoughts or people who create anxiety or stress.

My own defenses have sent me down the wrong path more than once. Although I didn't realize it at the time, my first significant use of these mechanisms was when I was a teenager, struggling to deal with my emotions around the turmoil in my home. Drugs and alcohol allowed me to avoid these painful feelings and escape the reality of my family drama. I spent all my time with my friends, who distracted me and made me feel good about myself. The result was prematurely leaving home and school, which had detrimental consequences.

We also use defense mechanisms in the corporate environment to avoid negativity or psychological harm. For example, if interactions with a boss or coworker creates undesirable emotions, such as self-doubt or fear, we may instinctively avoid those people.

Some of us may be able to resist these defensive drives, but when we are in a highly insecure state, I've found that our instinct to protect ourselves is strong and hard to resist. I experienced this after my partner passed away. I became avoidant of anything that challenged me or could create any further negativity.

Since these defenses are often driven by our subconscious, we may not realize we are using them. I learned this lesson when I looked back at my behaviors during that period of grief and saw how many of my actions had been instinctive, to protect my mental state, and not conscious choices. Due to my weakened condition, my subconscious worked harder to defend against perceived dangers. I truly hadn't been aware at the time that many of my decisions were driven by my need for protection.

These are the defense mechanisms that are most relevant to the topic of this book:

Anticipation

To ensure we are prepared to defend ourselves against any potential outcomes, we may anticipate and mentally prepare for all possibilities. This preparation is an attempt to reduce the risk of being caught off guard. We ask ourselves what if all possible outcomes occurred even though many of them could be very unlikely.

Having faced difficult experiences in my life and some completely unexpected, I tend to try and anticipate what will happen in the future. I have an innate need to create certainty for myself.

It takes considerable self-awareness and effort to control my use of this mechanism. I know I'm not alone in this challenge.

However, if we cannot overcome the tendency, it can waste time and distract us from more valuable pursuits. Energy is consumed considering risks that may never come to be. As said by the great Roman philosopher Seneca, "We suffer more often in imagination than in reality."

Denial

When we're in denial, we refuse to accept facts or see situations as they are. Healthy denial does serve a purpose in that we wouldn't function well if we focused on all the negative aspects of life, particularly the things that we have no control over. But it becomes detrimental when we deny information that could help us avoid a negative outcome.

I have seen those in denial ignore or doubt information that doesn't support their beliefs or desired outcome. For example, in the corporate world, this appears as looking for and seeing information that supports only the favored strategy.

Avoidance

Avoidance is a form of denial, but it's often action-oriented rather than purely a function of the mind. Using my life as an example, I used drugs and alcohol to actively avoid dealing with my family challenges. At work, an employee may avoid their boss rather than admit to them that they've made a mistake or missed a deadline. We use avoidance rather than dealing with unpleasant situations or people that could be harmful to our psyches.

Rationalization

We may rationalize an outcome or even our own behavior in ways that aren't altogether true. This creates comfort for us even if deep down we know something isn't right.

I've rationalized the conduct of a bullying boss, telling myself, "They didn't intend their words to be so hurtful," or "I'm just being oversensitive," to try and make the situation manageable. I've seen others do the same thing. We don't want to face that a work situation is truly indefensible and may require us to take difficult action. Regardless of our justification, the treatment will still hurt, and the rationalization can allow the conduct to continue.

Passive-Aggressive Behavior

People use passive-aggressive behavior to indirectly express anger, or unpopular or opposing opinions. If we fear confrontation, we may use passive-aggressive behaviors to get our point across while avoiding conflict. For example, we may make subtle comments to show our displeasure instead of directly saying we aren't happy, or we may accept responsibility for a task but then procrastinate about completing it.

Passive-aggressive behavior is often used since it's more socially acceptable than direct confrontation. However, it rarely leads to a positive outcome. The conduct simply wastes time, confuses people, and damages relationships.

Defense mechanisms are frequently referred to in the next two chapters where I outline the behaviors that occur when we're highly insecure. These behaviors negatively impact employee performance and working relationships.

I hope the last two introductory chapters have primed you to move into deeper material. These next sections should have you thinking about your conduct and the behaviors of others in a new light.

CHAPTER 3

INSECURITY AND EMPLOYEE PERFORMANCE

"Insecurity makes it difficult for us to make our voices heard, leaves us unable to dissent, and makes us tentative in our work relationships. It leaves us dissatisfied, undermines collaboration, and renders our teams less creative and efficient. If there is one enemy of authenticity and innovation, insecurity is it. No wonder we try so hard to get rid of it."

—WEBER AND PETRIGLIERI

Now to one of the questions this book aims to answer: does insecurity really impact employee performance and ultimately reduce profitability and growth? With absolute certainty, I can assure you that when insecurity reaches a high level, it does. The reality is, if protection of the psyche is someone's top priority, business objectives are not.

And I'm not referring only to poor performers who become highly insecure because they can't handle their workload. I'm talking about *any* employee. The hardest working and smartest people in your company can face uncertainties that lead to the unproductive behaviors we'll discuss.

High levels of insecurity might discourage those who could shine as top performers. Therefore, you need to end the conduct that magnifies insecurity and instead increase awareness and acceptance of the emotions we all feel.

This chapter looks at how insecurity deteriorates job performance; the following chapter discusses its impact on workplace relationships. You will recognize the behaviors in the stories I share, perhaps in your employees or even in yourself. Frequently, these reactions are defensive responses to perceived threats. The scenarios described are stark and negative, but they are also real and avoidable, so we must face them.

INABILITY TO FOCUS

This first story is about Christine, who became insecure due to the bullying of a new boss.

> Christine had joined her company fifteen months earlier as a sales manager. At that time, she reported to a boss who supported her growth. Under his leadership, she'd had great success as she mastered her role. However, he was promoted and replaced by a new sales director, Nicole.

Christine didn't expect a significant change since her role hadn't been altered, and if anything, given her proven successes, she thought Nicole might give her greater autonomy.

Before long, Christine discovered she was wrong. Nicole's leadership style was far different from her last boss; Nicole was a bully.

Nicole questioned every decision she made and pointed out any imperfections in her work. She also publicly discredited Christine.

In a sales manager meeting, Nicole questioned her experience. She asked if Christine had ever been in a sales manager role before this. Christine's current position was indeed her first role as a manager, but Nicole's intent of minimizing her to her peers was clear. The question was unnecessary in a team meeting and only served to make Christine feel inferior, since the other managers were more experienced in their roles.

Impeded by newly triggered insecurities, Christine began to take twice as long on tasks that she had been doing for a year. Yet, the increased time didn't add any value. She felt compelled to aim for perfection because she feared Nicole would publicly highlight any errors, no matter how small. Aiming for perfection on those tasks left little time for new sales efforts, so her sales numbers fell.

She struggled to stay focused on the work while her mind spun—about how to manage Nicole, whether she should stay or find another job, and how to avoid the further creation of self-doubt.

Within months, Christine had gone from enjoying her work and seeing a future with her company to waking up distracted and dreading what the day would bring.

In her insecure state, Christine's mind went on high alert against the threat that Nicole presented. Threats trigger an arousal response in our brains, activating our "fight or flight" instinct. As a reflex, we're given two options: to fight the threat or run away from it.

Christine was now focused on deciding if she should stay and "fight" in the toxic environment or move on and "flight" to a safer job elsewhere. This threat response is mentally draining, so it reduces productivity, limits analytical and creative thinking, and slows problem-solving abilities (Rock 2016).

Since threats also engage our defense mechanisms, we may try to anticipate every possible future outcome to prepare and protect. Christine's mind was trying to defend itself by figuring out how to manage Nicole and avoid any further damage.

In that state, the mind spins with anxiety about what *may* happen, stopping us from focusing on what *is* happening, missing details, missing deadlines, and not being present. Will my boss be satisfied? Will I be shamed in front of my peers again? Am I competent enough to do this work correctly?

Even the simple task of reading demonstrates the effect of this. We've all tried to read when our mind is elsewhere, and thoughts intrude; we must keep rereading sentences over and over for them to sink in.

You may have heard this referred to as mental chatter or other expressions, but psychologists refer to it formally as cognitive interference. Cognitive interference is when anxious, negative, preoccupying thoughts interrupt us as we're trying to complete a task, distracting us, and causing us to lose focus. Research has shown that this interference can reduce the quality and level of our performance (Sarason, Sarason, and Pierce 1995).

The inefficiency created by the interference will damage an employee's productivity. It also has the long-term effect of increasing our insecurity as we become disheartened by our performance.

The bottom line is that an anxious mind distracted by threats is not a high-performing mind. When our brains are battling this level of disturbance, we cannot perform to our full potential.

PROCRASTINATION

"You don't procrastinate to avoid work.
You do it to avoid negative emotions.
The task you're avoiding isn't always the one you hate.
Sometimes it's the one you fear."

—ADAM M. GRANT (@ADAMMGRANT MARCH 10, 2020)

We've all procrastinated when a task is unpleasant. Perhaps it's putting off a call, avoiding a tough conversation, or for some reason, being unable to write that important memo. We've all also been frustrated by peers who seem to be dragging their feet to complete tasks—in other words, procrastinating. We may even have judged peers as lazy or incompetent.

However, laziness often isn't the culprit. As we'll see in this next story, an employee may be trying to avoid a task that they just aren't comfortable with.

> As a product manager, Tom was required to submit his financial expectations by the end of the month. Budgeting and forecasting weren't Tom's strengths; he was insecure about his financial skills and anxious about his boss discovering his weakness.

Pressing customer issues kept coming up daily, and the task somehow slipped down Tom's priority list and kept slipping. The end of the day would come, and there wouldn't be time to pivot to the budget because he needed to leave work on time to pick up his kids.

As the month rolled on, Tom would lie in bed, each night pledging to himself that tomorrow he would get the budget done. Every morning, he'd be faced with a list of emails that needed to be answered before he could focus on the budget, and the end of the day would arrive before he knew it. All the while, the clock ticked toward the deadline.

Two days before the budget was due, Tom couldn't put off tackling it any longer. He finally opened the spreadsheet, only to realize that he didn't have the updated input costs from suppliers that were essential to completing the task. How was he going to get them in two days?

His stress level was now through the roof. He emailed his suppliers, imploring them to expedite information that would usually take them a week to compile, wasting a favor in the process.

Tom spent the next two days in a state of panic. He only managed to submit a subpar budget late on the night it was due. He received disappointed feedback from his boss that the budget lacked the needed detail. Tom's fear came to fruition; the budget submission impacted Tom's leader's perception of his abilities. This only furthered Tom's insecurity.

As we saw with Tom, if a task tests us or requires us to use a skill we're insecure about, we may procrastinate about completing it. In fact, research has demonstrated that insecurity is linked to procrastination (Sirois and Pychyl 2013).

Our instinct for self-preservation often drives us to find reasons and ways for the jobs that we find stressful to fall to the bottom of our priority list. This accomplishes hiding our perceived inadequacies, at least for the moment.

Unfortunately, the subconscious isn't particularly good at long-term thinking. It doesn't calculate that avoiding a task today will actually lead to greater mental pain later. It's programmed to avoid pain *now*, as if we were outrunning a dangerous animal. Logically, we may recognize that delaying the work is only going to hurt us, but this logic has to override the flight instinct in order to save the day.

If someone is waiting for us to complete a task, the pressure of knowing we may let them down will make the work seem even scarier. The effort builds up in our minds, becoming daunting.

This is impactful to companies because employees often don't fully process the effect of the procrastination on the business. They may avoid thinking about the result of their procrastination, just as they're avoiding the task with their procrastination. When the job is eventually completed, it may be late and of poor quality due to the rush when the work is finally done.

RISK AVERSION AND FEAR OF FAILURE

When we feel safe, we're more likely to take risks. We have confidence that we will succeed and overcome any challenges. In this section, I describe the behaviors that can occur when we *don't* feel this level of safety or confidence.

Fear of Change

The pace of technological innovation today is blistering. If companies don't evolve, they risk being bypassed by competitors. Product and process innovation is often necessary just to stay relevant. For companies to evolve, their workforce has to be open to change.

This next story shows what can happen to progress and innovation when employees fear change and don't feel safe taking risks.

> Company Z had been a successful business for over twenty years, but minimal evolution of their processes had occurred over that time.
>
> Company Z's services required that their customers share large amounts of their data. These customers were now demanding that Company Z undergo process automation to directly interface their systems with their customers'. Connecting these systems would eliminate the need to upload data files manually. This would also support real-time updates to Company Z's databases when customers made changes to their input data.
>
> The customers had evolved and taken advantage of technological advancements that would allow for this, but Company Z had not. Why was this?
>
> Company Z's CEO had an aggressive, often abusive, leadership style that played a part in the lack of innovation. He would publicly demean anyone who made a mistake or misjudgment. His toxic behavior created a workforce that was fearful of change. Employees weren't willing to risk the humiliation that would come if they failed or made mistakes—both of which are natural parts of innovation and growth.

Now, to avoid losing customers, Company Z was forced to pretend that they could handle the requested automation while implementing manual steps and quick Band-Aid solutions to manage the process. As with any manual processes or quick fixes, errors occurred.

Company Z was starting to lose its footing with their large accounts. Customers were leaving to competitors who had made the necessary upgrades. Company Z had missed their opportunity to evolve due to fear and the inaction it causes.

Company Z's employees are not alone in their avoidance of change when fearful. Humans have a natural tendency to stay with what is familiar to reduce risk, but this tendency is even more dominant in stressful situations (Greenberg 2018). This isn't exclusive to technological change either. Employees may not try different suppliers, or they may delay a decision, such as a new hire. They may avoid change in general, which includes innovation.

The defense mechanisms of denial and rationalization are often used in these situations to convince us that the perceived lower risk route is actually better for the organization. The employees of Company Z likely told themselves they were doing the right thing for the business by not evolving the processes. The subconscious mind can trick the conscious mind into believing almost anything if it serves to protect us.

Fear-Based Avoidance of Opportunities for Growth and Learning

Another effect of fear of failure has a less visible but nevertheless significant impact on business. If employees are insecure, they may be too fearful to challenge themselves and move their career forward.

Too often, insecurity holds people back from applying for promotions and even from accepting them when they are offered. Connie's story illustrates this.

Connie had been in her current role for two years. Although she didn't have formal education in her field, she was intelligent and had become highly proficient at her job; in addition, she was practical and had the common sense that many of her peers lacked. Her manager, Laurie, recognized that, with some training, Connie could be his successor. He had plans to advance up the company's career ladder. He approached Connie about it, but she shook her head and said, "No, no, I'm not the leadership type. I like being in the 'number two' role."

Laurie was perplexed. He'd grown up in an environment that instilled confidence and the belief that he was capable of anything. It was hard for him to understand how someone could reject an opportunity for career growth, particularly when it was handed to them on a silver platter.

The truth was that Connie had been affected by recent issues at the company; a number of significant changes, including layoffs, had shaken her sense of job security, making her extremely anxious. She was great at her current job, and that made her feel safe; she didn't want to do anything to risk losing that feeling.

At a deeper level, Connie felt inferior and unprepared because of her lack of relevant postsecondary education. She resisted the offered promotion because she was afraid that she might not rise to the challenge, fail, and lose her job.

She stayed in her mid-level position, continuing to turn down offers of education and career progression. Connie missed out on

> the opportunity for growth while her employer didn't benefit from the greater contribution that Connie could have provided.

For some people, like Connie, the possibility of failure is such a psychological threat that the motivation to avoid it is greater than the motivation to succeed.

You may know people with a lot of potential and actual accomplishments who stay in the same job forever. You can't understand why they aren't growing their career. Their self-doubt may be what's holding them back.

When I was offered my first promotion (from receptionist to administrative assistant), my insecurity and self-doubt nearly stopped me from taking it. I hadn't progressed my education yet, and I genuinely felt that I "wasn't good enough" for a promotion. I felt safe in my current role and was nervous about risking that feeling of safety.

Fortunately, I had a boss who saw what I was capable of and pushed me to stretch my abilities. If it hadn't been for her, I might never have taken that critical step. Unfortunately, many people aren't as lucky as I was and don't have a mentor to help them overcome their fears. Even worse, toxic leaders or environments may magnify employees' self-doubt and exacerbate their aversions.

As a result, companies don't benefit from the potential of people already inside their organizations. Businesses incur the recruitment and training costs of hiring externally when they have talent right in front of them.

Like the way Connie's fear held back her growth, the fear of failure can create a reluctance to learn. At the best of times, anxiety can make us nervous about trying something unfamiliar. But if we are highly insecure, the low self-esteem that goes hand in hand with insecurity can magnify this natural anxiety. We may avoid even trying to learn as we assume we will fail.

I've found myself reluctant to attempt even straightforward new experiences like playing a basic sport because my overall confidence was low. A subconscious unwillingness stopped me from trying, and self-doubt told me I wouldn't be any good and failing would heighten my insecurity.

When we are already insecure, our subconscious doesn't want to risk further damage by trying to learn and failing, thereby proving that our fear of being unable to learn is right—the validation of what we believe is an inherent weakness would be more than we could take.

An organization that doesn't create a secure environment for growth and learning will face limitations in internal promotion and succession planning. Internal candidates may not be prepared for advancement if they haven't been encouraged to develop their skills.

FEAR OF INFORMATION SHARING
AND COLLABORATION

There's real vulnerability in openly speaking our minds. That feeling of vulnerability can be magnified if people have reacted negatively to what we, or others, have said or even to the fact that we spoke up at all. As I'll discuss in this section, these negative reactions, which may extend to shaming or demeaning us, can engender deep insecurity. Such insecurity can make us increasingly fearful and unwilling to speak up or collaborate with our peers. It can also lead employees to withhold information or even lie as a means of self-protection.

Fear of Speaking Up

This next story highlights the impact when a leader demeans individuals to control a meeting.

> Gary wanted his project meetings to run as efficiently as possible. This meant that he would shut down anyone who asked a question that he didn't view as useful or relevant to the group or that he simply didn't like.
>
> After a few people tried to ask a question or start a discussion on a topic and were demeaned for "distracting" the group, everyone learned to stay quiet. The meetings devolved into a series of feed-forward update presentations of project status with no Q&A.
>
> The meetings should have been opportunities for peers to learn from one another, offer insights, and inspire creativity. Instead, Gary's need to keep the meetings on track and under his control made the sessions a waste of time. The same limited level of benefit could have been achieved by simply sending the PowerPoint presentations to everyone with a summary.
>
> Yet, these meetings continued. Gary had created a threatening work environment where people were too afraid (or too disaffected by the dismissive treatment) to ask questions. And absolutely no one was willing to contribute the observation that an e-mail would have the same effect as the meetings with less time wasted.

In a threatening situation like the one Gary created, anyone would be cautious before speaking up, regardless of their confidence level. There's risk in being open and sharing ourselves, particularly if we have seen others who do speak up get slapped down.

As Amy Edmondson (2011), a Harvard Business School professor and author of *The Fearless Organization*, found in her research, people decide whether to share their thoughts by first assessing the situation (often subconsciously) and then calculating whether it's worth the interpersonal risk to speak up.

Our past experiences feed into this calculation. If we see too many red flags, we keep our thoughts to ourselves. Often, many of us do the mental math and opt out of sharing our thoughts. In fact, one survey found that 40 percent of respondents said they don't feel confident sharing their ideas at work (Hurt and Dye 2020). That's a lot of people doing the mental calculation and deciding it's better to keep their thoughts to themselves.

Many times throughout my career, I didn't voice my opinion or I held back my words because I didn't feel safe. Sometimes this was because of my own personal insecurities, but often it was because the environment was objectively threatening due to the conduct of leaders or peers.

In one workplace, my manager tended to pick favorites, so my colleagues had developed a habit of jockeying to overshadow one another to win favor. If someone threw out an idea, someone else was always at the ready to cut it down or try to one-up the idea. I don't think the behavior was personally targeted at anyone because everyone was just looking out for the safety of their jobs, but it had the result of silencing me and many of my peers.

When we know an idea is likely to be rejected or a question ridiculed, the instinct is to protect ourselves by staying silent.

In a threatening work environment, only the people who are extremely secure and those whose need for validation from speaking overpowers the potential risk will share their thoughts. Businesses are likely to stagnate when this occurs. Asking questions clarifies instructions, fleshes out ideas, suggests novel approaches to solving problems, and leads to learning for everyone. This organizational openness is essential for innovation and growth.

Reluctance to Collaborate

Along with the reluctance to share ideas or ask questions when we're feeling highly insecure, we're also much less likely to seek the opinions of others on our decisions or strategies. In this next story, James's fear of negative feedback from his peers stopped him from collaborating to gain buy-in.

> As the head of finance for his company, James's highest priority goal for the year was to implement a modern purchase order system. The implementation would require the support of his fellow department heads because the tool would be used company-wide.
>
> However, the organization had an extremely dysfunctional culture. Backstabbing, passive aggressiveness, and other toxic behaviors were common. Even though James knew he needed to consult his peers before selecting a solution, he couldn't bring himself to deal with the likely negative opinions and critical feedback.
>
> Instead, he rationalized that all purchase order technologies were essentially the same; he'd implemented them for former employers, so he had the knowledge to make the choice.
>
> James was correct that he could make the right decision on his own. However, his rationalization overlooked that he needed all department heads to actively support the change, to encourage their teams to attend training, and use the new system.

He launched the tool (which was first rate and perfect for the company), but his peers shunned it. They were offended that they hadn't been asked for their opinion on the tool. James ended up having to deal with the negative feedback that he'd been trying to avoid and, far worse, the failure of the launch.

Most of us have had times where we feared the critique of our decisions and therefore "kept our cards close to our chest" to protect our ideas and ourselves. However, when employees don't share their ideas and plans out of self-protection, the result can be that the best strategy is never identified.

There's great value in bouncing ideas around with peers. Talking through a strategy with coworkers can improve the strategy through their added insight. A better idea may come to light through team brainstorming. At a minimum, valuable learning occurs when team members share information and buy-in is increased when people feel involved. A company that doesn't create a safe environment for collaboration risks poorly considered strategies and failed projects.

Omitting Information and Lying

"Many lies are the product of insecurity.
These are lies motivated by fear, and they provide
temporary psychological protection
to the liar's ego."

—Tomas Chamorro-Premuzic

The fear created in a toxic work environment can have impacts beyond simply not sharing thoughts and ideas. It can prompt an employee to lie about or omit information if they sense the outcome of sharing that information could cause psychological harm.

In the next story, Lane was driven to hide his oversight because of his intense fear of his boss's anger.

> Lane was the Accounts Payable manager at Company J. He prided himself on being up front and honest with everyone he spoke to.
>
> Lane's boss asked him if he had talked to a supplier to confirm that recent invoices were correct. Lane quickly replied that he had. But after he walked away from the conversation, Lane realized that in fact he hadn't spoken to the supplier yet and that he'd lied reflexively. Lane's boss had a history of frighteningly angry outbursts whenever something didn't happen according to his timeline. Without any conscious thought, Lane had lied to protect himself.
>
> Lane texted his boss right away, telling him he had been mixed up and had not spoken to the supplier yet. (Texting avoided a personal confrontation.)
>
> Lane was deeply disturbed that his boss's behavior had this effect on him. But he'd tried to find a job elsewhere with no success, and so he felt resigned to staying at Company J. He felt trapped; his engagement diminished.

In this instance, Lane's lie didn't have a detrimental effect on Company J's business. But if the information in question is important to management's decision-making process, the impact of an employee withholding or misrepresenting information could be significant.

Decision making in the absence of complete information can be dangerous. If the decision maker isn't aware of the information gap, they can't mitigate the risk the gap presents. Case in point: An employee self-protectively withholds the information that a major customer is very unhappy and is considering going to a competitor. As a result, the company's leaders make financial plans that don't factor in this potential loss of revenue. Without the information, management also loses the opportunity to take action to keep the customer and possibly avoid the loss.

A less dramatic situation is when an employee is too fearful to be open about their lack of skills and/or experience that is essential for performing a task. Unaware of those issues, their manager may give them too much responsibility or not enough support from experienced staff. The result is poor performance and possibly the failure to achieve an objective or meet a goal.

This self-protective behavior has a short-term payoff to the individual in that an immediate confrontation or rejection is avoided. Unfortunately, this is short-term thinking that can have longer-term repercussions to the business *and* the employee.

If the omission or lie is discovered, it can cause a greater loss of faith in the individual than if the truth had been shared in the first place.

MISSED OPPORTUNITIES, WINS, AND POSITIVES

When we are an insecure state, we may not see the very things that could improve our outlook. The next story, set during the COVID-19 pandemic, demonstrates this. Crises are challenging situations with threats and risks; however, most situations have alternatives that can mitigate the damage if companies have employees who are able to see them.

When his city went on lockdown to stop the spread of the COVID virus, the restaurant that Bruce managed was required to stop dine-in service. However, pickups and deliveries were still permitted.

Unfortunately, Bruce had a poor relationship with the owners of the restaurant. He was insecure about the safety of his job and looking at the business, and the world, through a negative lens. He could only see the worst outcome from the pandemic and was too afraid to think outside the box.

Bruce advised the restaurant owners that he didn't see a good alternative to closing the restaurant. They decided to lay off all employees and board up the business to wait it out.

Meanwhile, Bob, another restaurant manager in the same city, was in a more secure mental state. His positive mindset enabled him to assess the situation creatively.

He was faced with the same lockdown and potential staff layoffs (a few had already been furloughed). But he recognized that people who couldn't leave their homes and had limited entertainment options would order meals for delivery to provide some novelty. Bob's restaurant website wasn't set up for ordering, but he thought it would be worth investing in this functionality.

Bob had a positive relationship with the owners, so he felt safe sharing his ideas, and they accepted them. Bob adjusted the menu to suit in-home delivery and pickup and hired a web designer to set up online ordering. He also opened accounts with delivery apps to build the restaurant's name. His judgment was correct: the takeout side of the business generated sufficient revenues for the restaurant to remain open, and furloughed staff were brought back.

By creating an intimidating working relationship with Bruce, the restaurant owners had produced a situation in which their most important employee, who otherwise would have been alert to ways to preserve the business, was psychologically hobbled. Bob's employers, who had maintained a positive working relationship with him, were the beneficiaries of his insight: a revenue stream that got the restaurant through a challenging time so that it could prosper in the future. The comparison of Bob's and Bruce's stories demonstrates the profoundly different outcomes that can develop out of the same situation when it's processed through an insecure-negative mindset versus a secure-positive one.

Establishing a positive mindset, in yourself as a leader and in the employees in your organization, isn't easy, in part because of some hardwired human nature. Research has shown that in general, people are more sensitive and reactive to situations they perceive as negative than to those they perceive as positive (Baumeister et al. 2001). This tendency is referred to as the negativity bias.

Alertness to dangers and threats no doubt conferred evolutionary benefits by protecting humans in life-and-death situations (Cherry 2020). However, the modern result of this innate self-protectiveness is that our brains are attuned to spot the negative aspects of a situation *first*: the greater our sense of insecurity, the more we will be on the lookout for threats. Like Bruce, our heightened sense of imminent danger may block us from seeing the upside to situations. In a toxic, threatening workplace, it can be difficult for even the most self-aware person to manage their negativity bias and see the positives.

When I was in such an environment, I had to consciously turn my mind away from the negatives to ensure I also gave weight to the positives. I would go as far as making a list of the good and bad points of a situation so that I had a visual to refer to and my mind couldn't trick me into focusing only on the threats.

In business, employees must constantly process and assess information, whether fact or rumor, about changes in their industry and in the world in general. In any emotional state, we will have bias toward some information over others, so it's always a challenge to properly digest what we hear, read, and see. With a heightened negativity bias, the challenge is even greater. The bias can lead to a self-fulfilling prophecy of poor results from missed opportunities and potential wins.

The negativity bias not only affects a workforce's ability to assess factors external to the business, but as shown in the next story of Company T, it can also have a profound effect on the establishment and maintenance of a positive corporate culture.

After over ten years of success, Company T was acquired. The change was exciting for employees but also created apprehension. Company T had an excellent culture, and the staff felt like a family. They were nervous the new owners might impose undesirable changes.

Company T's CEO, Jason, was led to believe by the acquiring company that the culture could be maintained. Jason shared those assurances with his team—things would stay the same and now the business would be well funded for growth and innovation. Jason honestly believed this, and because of the employees' deep trust in him, they believed it, too.

But before long and despite all assurances to the contrary, the financial demands and regulatory obligations asserted by the acquirer made organizational changes inevitable and unavoidable.

Jason fought for his employees, but the parent company's financial targets couldn't be met with Company T's existing corporate structure. Major changes were imposed, constraining Jason's authority, redefining roles and processes, dismantling teams, and laying off a significant number of employees. Those who weren't laid off felt survival guilt for being spared in an environment that had rejected their friends.

It was extremely painful for Jason to watch the impact on his team, and he was deeply unhappy with the constraints on his ability to make decisions. After a year, he resigned, feeling that he was no longer the right leader for the business. The employees felt bereft at losing the leader they trusted, but they understood why he wouldn't want to continue working within the new structure.

The parent company brought in a new CEO, Sarah, to run Company T. Sarah was aware of the deteriorating morale and tried to revive the culture by rolling out positive improvements. However, every time changes were announced, employees seemed to only notice and comment on aspects they perceived as negative.

In one such instance, the announced changes included four generous adjustments to benefits, such as a new $500-a-year fitness allowance and a 50 percent increase in funding for their existing education reimbursement program. However, this same announcement contained one change that could be perceived as negative: the number of days employees could work from home was limited to three a week, and those days had to be planned at least a week ahead of time. Sarah received no comments or morale win from the four positive changes. The only responses and discussion at the next town hall meeting were about the unfairness of the work-from-home policy.

As a result of the post-acquisition changes, the employees had become deeply insecure. Their vigilance for negative changes was heightened. Their negativity bias blinded them to any good outcomes, making it extremely difficult for Sarah to break through and rebuild.

This negative bias continued for many years post-acquisition. Sarah was unsuccessful with reigniting positivity in many employees. She was forced to replace a lot of the staff as their negativity resulted in poor performance or they self-selected and left the company. The turnover was significant in the year after Jason left. And despite positive changes, it failed to level off, maintaining a high rate the following year until most of the team was made up of new hires.

Due to the impact of the negativity bias and the challenge of addressing it once it had set in, Company T lost many years of institutional knowledge, product-specific expertise, and valuable relationships with customers. Further, it incurred significant recruitment and training costs. The acquisition never met expectations, and within five years of the original acquisition, the parent company divested itself of Company T.

The story of Company T demonstrates how, when changes to an existing positive corporate culture are imposed from outside it, the resulting insecurity and negative biases among the employees can be detrimental to the bottom line for a long time afterward.

Company T not only lost critical knowledge, but its innovation and growth also slowed. Although the parent company (through Sarah) put effort into perks, insecurity and negativity were too deeply ingrained in the workforce. Positive changes weren't recognized as such.

I've witnessed this in multiple organizations when, after difficult changes and layoffs, staff have been unable to recover and trust the management team. In some cases, employees do eventually open themselves up to the opportunities within a new structure, but it takes effort by leaders; too often, significant contributors leave the company before the intense negativity bias can be overcome.

AVOIDANCE OF
NEGATIVE INFORMATION

Many of us will react to a threatening environment by hyperfocusing on potential risks. However, others will instead respond by either avoiding or completely denying negative information that, if acknowledged, would increase our feelings of fear and insecurity about the situation.

In this next story, Dan's project manager, Pat, reacted to his stress and insecurity with avoidance of any negative information about their project. Ultimately, that avoidance resulted in a worse outcome than if he had faced the situation directly.

> Dan was hired by Company D as a project analyst to join the team working on a time-sensitive project. Right away, he noticed that every project meeting was about exceeding targets and beating deadlines. However, outside of the meetings, he saw missed targets, unacknowledged financial constraints, and stressed-out employees.
>
> Dan privately asked a coworker why the difference existed and was told that Pat didn't want to hear about problems. Pat was managing multiple projects and was stressed by the heavy

workload. He'd also made some mistakes recently and so was feeling insecure. Any bad news threatened to further damage his mental state, so he made efforts to avoid it. As a result, Pat had reacted with frustration and anger when employees informed him of problems.

The team clearly read what Pat's response implied: he didn't want to hear about any issues with the project. Pat's avoidant behavior effectively shifted the team's cultural norm to one in which they talked about only the good news with him in public and saved the problems for discussion among themselves. This outcome was negatively impacting the project because Pat, as team leader, was neither addressing problems as they arose nor making decisions on the basis of a fully informed assessment of challenges.

Dan didn't want to continue working on a project that felt like a ticking time bomb. He found a job elsewhere and resigned.

On his last day, he met with Pat and told him that he wasn't hearing what was really happening on the project. Pat waved away the report and changed the subject. He clearly didn't want to hear what Dan had to say.

Dan later heard that in the end, the project was delivered nine months late and 100 percent over budget.

It's not uncommon to seek out uplifting information to improve our mindset. This isn't necessarily negative; there's generally so much depressing information in our world today that finding good news can be a tool in consciously cultivating a positive outlook.

However, Pat's negative reaction when his team delivered him bad news didn't have a positive effect for this team: it made them insecure. I have seen teams pick up on avoidance or denial by their leaders and become reluctant to disclose negative information for fear of the reaction. Pat's team reacted in this manner, avoiding him and withholding information to protect themselves from his anger. You'll recognize that this also created the situation I described earlier under "Omitting Information and Lying."

Unfortunately, when people are afraid to raise business problems, issues aren't addressed, leading to negative outcomes like the late delivery and blown budget on Pat's project.

WHY THIS MATTERS TO YOU

Lower Productivity

When people are insecure, their anxiety reduces their ability to focus on their work and increases their tendency toward procrastination and avoidance. Work tasks will take longer to complete, and productivity will drop. In all companies, time is money, so the employees must be functioning at optimal efficiency. An organization with an insecure workforce will never reach peak productivity.

Lack of Innovation

If employees are fearful of change, of taking risks, or of sharing their thoughts, the generation of new ideas for innovative products or process improvements will be lower. This puts a business's competitive advantage at risk.

Limited Succession Planning

An organization that doesn't create a secure environment in which employees are willing to take risks will face challenges with succession planning. Those who logically should be internal candidates may be fearful to accept promotions. Additionally, employees may be unprepared for advancement because they haven't taken opportunities to learn and grow due to their fear of failure.

Limited Collaboration

Great business decisions emerge from discussions that engage all the relevant stakeholders. Collaboration will be inhibited when insecure employees are fearful of sharing their thoughts, plans, and opinions with others. This can limit the success of change initiatives that require prior collaboration to obtain buy-in.

Lost Opportunities

For businesses to succeed, employees must recognize opportunities and have the confidence to take advantage of them. A negativity bias will make it difficult for an insecure leadership team and/or workforce to see opportunities. They will be too focused on threats. If they do see the opportunities, self-doubt may make them too fearful to capitalize on them. The company will miss out on potential wins.

Reduced Awareness of Organizational Issues

When employees are insecure, they are less likely to share information with their managers and are more likely to omit or even lie about information that they feel may cause them harm. And insecure leaders may be avoidant, if only on a subconscious level, of seeing and hearing negative information. The combination of these factors may blind leaders to issues within an organization until it's too late to make adjustments because the detrimental effects have already occurred.

CHAPTER 4

INSECURITY AND WORK RELATIONSHIPS

Insecurity can diminish our natural tendencies, silencing extroverts and hindering otherwise great communicators and collaborators. The instinct to protect ourselves can cause us to hide and act in ways that don't reflect who we really are. When we aren't ourselves and driven by defensive mechanisms, working relationships can be damaged or it can be difficult to establish relationships at all.

This chapter will discuss the insecure behaviors that can harm workplace dynamics and distort our views of one another. The stories shared will demonstrate that high levels of insecurity can elicit conduct that shuts down the sharing of information, allows bullying to occur, and creates harmful conflict between employees.

COMPARISON AND JEALOUSY

"Comparison is the thief of joy."

—Theodore Roosevelt

We've all experienced at least a twinge of jealousy when someone has something that we don't or has achieved something that we would like to accomplish ourselves. From a young age, we may have experienced jealousy when someone's natural abilities surpassed ours or when someone's parents bought them the latest toy that our own parents couldn't afford.

As shown in this next story, feelings of jealousy can manifest in the work setting as well, even at the leadership levels of businesses.

Lily and Heather were both department heads in their organization and had teams involved in the same important project. The department heads met regularly on the project's progress. Attendance at these sessions was the means for every department head to keep their team's contributions aligned with the project plan and to properly contribute the perspective of their department.

Heather, who had taken on the responsibility for booking the meetings, left Lily off the invitation list for a meeting, and Lily missed it. When Lily called Heather about the situation, Heather said that the omission had been accidental. Then it happened again. And two weeks later, again. It was apparent to Lily that this probably wasn't an accident.

Heather was deeply insecure because of a recent promotion into a position she wasn't ready for. Heather compared herself to Lily, who had more years of experience and education in her field than Heather had in hers. Lily also had close working relationships with the senior executives on the project. Heather felt jealous and threatened.

Because of the scheduling incidents, Lily now distrusted Heather but still had to have a functional working relationship with her, both because of the immediate project and their respective roles in the business.

Lily then noticed that Heather was failing to provide her with departmental updates that impacted Lily's team.

As leaders of their departments, the unease in their relationship spread to interactions between their team members as well. This created dysfunction between their departments, which was detrimental to the business.

Lily eventually left the organization. The interaction with Heather was a symptom of overall cultural issues in the company that Lily didn't think would change.

Research has directly linked the feeling of jealousy to a sense of inferiority and insecurity (Salovey and Rodin 1984). Our self-doubt can cause us to see only what other people have that we don't, rather than what we *do* have.

I have seen insecure employees so bothered by the success of peers at work that they became obsessive about their perceived rival. Instead of celebrating their colleague's wins and welcoming the opportunity to learn from them, they felt shame that they hadn't achieved the same success and became deeply resentful.

In extreme cases, the resentment and jealousy can drive the person, consciously or subconsciously, to go as far as undermining their peer's successes in order to shore up their shaky self-confidence.

Lily experienced this outcome when Heather excluded her from significant meetings.

I once experienced this myself, when I was given a challenging new responsibility by my manager. At first, they were very supportive of expanding my skillset. However, I was more successful than they'd anticipated. When I received significant public positive feedback for my work, my boss's tone changed. They weren't getting similar positive feedback. All of a sudden, they didn't feel I was the right person for the task after all, and so it should be given to others on our team instead.

In this case, jealousy not only smothered my potential success and growth, but the task also went to employees who may not have been as successful as I was in the effort. It wasn't good for the business.

Jealousy motivates two additional toxic behaviors: disparagement and distancing (Mennon and Thompson 2010). Disparagement is the minimization by one individual of another's success, stating or implying that it's less than it appears or is the result of favoritism. Overt disparagement can be as harmful as shaming the other person publicly; alternatively, the disparagement may be confined to the mind of the jealous individual as they make themselves feel better by telling themselves that the rival isn't as talented as everyone thinks. Distancing is the desire of the jealous person to no longer work with, collaborate with, or learn from their rival. Both behaviors damage relationships, disrupt teams, and undermine company performance through missed opportunities and organizational inefficiency.

PASSIVE-AGGRESSIVE BEHAVIOR

Passive-aggressive behavior can emerge when we are too fearful to openly give our opinions or express our feelings. In the work context, we may fear a backlash from a leader or coworker if we disagree directly or raise opposing points to their perspectives.

I described passive-aggressive behavior in the earlier discussion of defense mechanisms; I'm raising it again here because it's highly prevalent in the workplace. (If we're being honest with ourselves, it's prevalent in all parts of life.)

Lois's story demonstrates the impact that this behavior can have at work.

Lois's coworker, John, who was senior to her in the company, wanted Lois to add a step to their banking process. He proposed that she print all banking receipts and file them in an office cabinet. He explained that he hadn't been able to find a receipt electronically and thought this would help.

Lois didn't think this made sense. The receipts were well organized on the network drive; she concluded that John's incident was a one-off misfiling event. And shouldn't the business be limiting printing and trying to be greener?

John had brought up the process change repeatedly in emails. Given that John had greater authority in the organization than Lois, she didn't want to start a conflict with him, so she ignored his attempts to discuss the topic and continued following the existing process.

John became quite annoyed that Lois was answering other emails from him but ignoring the ones in which he asked for the process change. He decided to raise it at the next team meeting. When he did, Lois said that she didn't have time to discuss the process as she had a call and ducked away.

John was starting to think that Lois was lazy and didn't want the extra work. After a number of days had gone by, John finally stopped Lois in the hall and asked her, mildly but directly, why she was avoiding him on the topic.

Now that they were face-to-face, Lois could no longer try to make the issue go away by ignoring it. She explained her reasoning: the electronic files were well organized and they were probably dealing with a case of one-off human error; this being the case, she didn't think it made sense to change the whole process over one missing receipt. She added that printing documents didn't align with the company's environmental values statement. Instead, she proposed that going forward, they tag each payment with the name of the payee rather than just the date, as they had been doing, to make it easier to find the documents.

John immediately understood her point and good-naturedly admitted that he hadn't thought about it that way. "Why didn't you just tell me that?" he asked. Lois's fear of conflict had caused unnecessary tension in their relationship when her opinion was valid all along.

Passive-aggressive behaviors like Lois's can have many undesirable effects. Although insecure people who are afraid to act directly often use the approach, the fact is that it can also magnify any insecurities in the person on the receiving end of the conduct. When someone uses passive-aggressive tactics, it creates uncertainty about what their intentions are. As I will discuss in later chapters, uncertainty can trigger insecurity. In Lois's case, John didn't know if she was being lazy, wasn't getting his messages, or if there was some other reason for her avoidance.

Passive-aggressive behavior also results in the misalignment of words and actions. The person may say they support a plan, but then their actions indicate otherwise. This misalignment is confusing and disorienting for the person trying to understand it.

In the case of Lois and John, their core relationship was solid enough that when he asked her face-to-face what was going on, she trusted him sufficiently to answer directly, and that led to resolving the issue to their mutual satisfaction.

Needless to say, this conduct is most prevalent in toxic environments where perceived threats make speaking up too risky, so the behavior is used to signal dissatisfaction or avoid an unwanted outcome. In that environment, employees aren't comfortable being straightforward. The resulting poor communication can result in permanent rifts between coworkers.

Examples of workplace passive-aggressive behavior (some of which Lois exhibited) are:

- Opposing a plan but rather than communicating this directly, dragging one's feet or throwing up roadblocks
- Being deliberately inefficient and ignoring deadlines
- Ignoring statements rather than dealing with them
- Limiting access to information or processes that would move the offending issue forward
- Refusing to discuss topics and using the silent treatment
- Resorting to backhanded compliments

In addition to heightening the insecurity of those involved, these behaviors harm productivity by delaying the identification of problems and the resolution of them. Directness brings light to challenges, speeding up the decision-making process and enabling faster identification of workable solutions.

AVOIDANCE OF INTERPERSONAL INTERACTION

In my experience, there's a tendency to turn inward and avoid social interaction when struggling with insecurity. This outcome is shown in the next story of Mark, normally a social person, who was too weakened by the treatment of his bullying boss to risk social situations in a toxic work environment.

> Mark was recruited into the role of IT manager at Company P. He had the technical skills for the role, but his calm, friendly demeanor is what made him stand out against other candidates. The company's once-healthy culture needed a boost of positive energy. It had deteriorated recently, and staff turnover was on the rise. However, the primary reason the corporate culture was suffering was the effect of toxic conduct by some of its leaders; unfortunately, Mark reported to one of these leaders.
>
> By the time he was six months into his role, Mark had suffered through multiple bullying and demeaning interactions with his boss. Mark's once-outgoing and chatty demeanor all but disappeared.
>
> It took all of his energy to prepare for and guard himself against the toxic behavior of his leader. He stopped attending company social events and didn't engage with his peers outside

of meetings. He isolated himself as protection from the threats in the toxic environment.

Mark eventually saw what the toxicity was doing to him, so he quit his job after two years. Looking back now, he wished he'd left much sooner.

By failing to intervene to halt the bullying conduct of its leaders, Company P missed out on the positive effect that Mark could have had on their corporate culture, and they ultimately lost him as an employee as well.

In general, if we're highly insecure, we'll self-protectively avoid any situation that could make us feel worse about ourselves. It's a fact of life that sometimes people can say things or do things that hurt us. If we're already hurt, we'll avoid further damage by limiting social interaction.

I've worked in companies with healthy cultures. There, people looked up as I walked by, made eye contact, smiled, and said hello.

In the toxic workplaces that I've experienced, only those who were highly extroverted still sought interaction, their need for connection seemed to overpower any insecurity they were feeling. Most employees kept their heads down, not risking unnecessary contacts because their instincts told them that the environment was dangerous. When I'd walk through those offices, they were silent; no one looked up or made eye contact. The difference was stark.

This avoidance of social interaction can damage work performance because it stops employees from building relationships with coworkers. Rather than interact directly with colleagues, those who are avoidant may choose less efficient ways to get work done—for example, sending an email when a quick phone call could have gotten the response right away or researching a solution when someone else knew the answer and would have provided it if asked.

When a culture has become toxic, efforts to turn it around and create a positive and engaged corporate environment will encounter the challenge of this social avoidance. Leaders will need to rebuild a sense of security before employees will be willing to put themselves at risk and increase interactions.

INABILITY TO STAND UP TO BULLIES

"Insecure people have a special sensitivity
for anything that finally confirms their
low opinion of themselves."

—SUE GRAFTON

Sadly, when we are insecure, we are less likely to stand up to bullies. The following story illustrates this reality.

> After being out of the workforce for some time, Walter joined a new company as a department head. He felt a bit rusty and insecure. Unfortunately, he reported to Richard, who was a bully to compensate for his own insecurities.
>
> Richard didn't give Walter any credit for his past work experience and the insights that Walter could bring to the job. Instead, he wanted Walter to do the work exactly as he himself would do it. If Walter did any task differently, Richard would yell and slam his fists on the table. Walter made small mistakes while he tried to learn the role, and upon discovering them, Richard ridiculed him in front of his peers. The micromanaging and bullying were so intense that

Walter began taking antianxiety medications before every meeting with Richard and avoiding interactions with him whenever possible.

Every month, Walter received a cost report for his department from the accountant via email. Richard was cc'd on the messages. After a couple of months of this bullying, when Walter responded with questions, he removed Richard from the email chain. He didn't want to risk saying or asking anything that would set Richard off. This is just one example of how Walter worked to avoid his boss rather than stand up to him.

Eventually, Walter resigned and reported Richard's behavior in his exit interview. Walter only worked up the confidence to speak up after he heard that another employee had also reported Richard for bullying. Up until that point, Walter's insecurity had created self-doubt and thoughts that he deserved this treatment. The knowledge that someone else had put their foot down gave him the courage to do the same.

Often when we feel insecure, we lack clear personal boundaries or the ability to establish them. When our protective interpersonal boundaries are low, we're vulnerable; we take feedback personally, and pushing back is a struggle (McKeown 2014). In that state, we may avoid a bully and work around them rather than face or report them; the response can ultimately damage our work performance. This is exactly what Walter experienced when he tried to cope with his bullying boss through antianxiety medication and avoidance before finally resigning.

I went through a period in my career in which, like Walter, I allowed a workplace bully to damage my life for a period. This individual micromanaged my work and the work of my team. If

I didn't complete my tasks exactly as the bully wanted, I received abuse. They would ask me about specific technical details of areas in which they knew I was inexperienced to undermine my confidence. They'd point out imperfections in my work, reacting harshly to inconsequential mistakes or omissions; they were intensely critical and left me no room for explanations. And they hounded me outside of working hours, emailing and messaging in the early morning, in the evening, and on weekends.

I found out that this leader had a long history of bullying that included even worse conduct than what I was experiencing. I also learned that their behavior was known to those who had placed them in their position. I became insecure and too scared to set boundaries and report the bully. After months of trying to manage the stress, I finally chose to leave the organization. I realized that any company that accepted that conduct was not one I wanted to be part of.

Apart from being afraid the individual's bullying behavior would escalate, I also let the treatment go on for too long because the bully's harsh words made me doubt myself. If we're filled with self-doubt, we're likely to believe insults, even thinking that we deserve poor treatment. We start to second-guess ourselves even more than usual. We question whether the bully is right: that all our past successes have been dumb luck. This self-questioning only increases our insecurity and the manifestation of the behaviors discussed in this chapter.

Fortunately, while I was working for the bully, I had positive relationships with peers at work and in my personal life. When I told my confidantes about this abuse, they all advised me to get out. They saw the impact it had on me. They helped me to see that I didn't deserve the abusive treatment and that it wasn't acceptable;

they also made me see that if the bully had gotten away with such conduct for as long as I'd been told, the situation wasn't going to improve.

Unfortunately, many people don't have support or the flexibility to resign from their positions. This is why companies need to take action to stop bullying behaviors and ensure it's clear to all in their organization that the conduct is unacceptable. Too many people suffer in silence, harming their quality of life and reducing their ability to contribute at work.

DEFENSIVENESS AND EASILY TRIGGERED ANGER

Managing performance and providing constructive feedback aren't easy. The challenge is even greater when the employee receiving the feedback is insecure.

In this next story, Jake learned this when he attempted to give constructive feedback to Russell.

Company A had been through a difficult year. It had lost two of its largest customers; to balance the revenue shortfall, many employees had been let go. Those who remained felt deeply insecure, worrying that the same could happen to them.

Jake, a leader at Company A, was having trouble with one of his team members, Russell. Russell was frequently coming into the office late; his coworkers often needed his help first thing in the morning and he wasn't there to provide it.

Jake sat down with Russell to discuss his tardiness and ask how he could support Russell to correct the problem. Russell instantly became defensive. He turned the feedback around and stated accusingly that Jake was often late, too. In essence, Russell denied that his lateness was a problem because Jake did the same thing. Jake hadn't expected this result, and he also became defensive.

The quality of the discussion rapidly deteriorated. They both raised their voices and stopped hearing each other. The exchange was interrupted by a coworker, warning them that their voices could be heard down the hall. They ended the meeting with no resolution.

Jake didn't have the skills to manage Russell's defensive reaction, so going forward, he ignored the situation. Russell continued to be late, and the tension on the team grew. In the absence of any further effort by Jake to manage his performance, Russell's defiant behavior only increased. After months of this impasse, Russell was finally let go.

In this story Russell, who was insecure due to layoffs in the company, became defensive. I've had many real-world performance discussions with employees and have observed that when people are highly insecure, constructive feedback is often perceived as a threat.

In Chapter 3, I discussed how perceived threats cause us to lose focus on anything other than the threat, and our fight-or-flight reaction is triggered. "Fight" can manifest as defensiveness.

Daniel Goleman (1995) discusses this emotional reaction in his book *Emotional Intelligence: Why It Can Matter More than IQ*, dubbing it the "amygdala hijack." The amygdala is the part of the brain in which emotions are assigned meaning, remembered, and responses to them generated. It plays a significant role in our response to fear. If we feel that negative feedback from our leader will harm our psyche, out of fear, our amygdala may send a message to put up our defenses.

Research has shown that if we are under stress, it becomes easier to trigger this reaction resulting in more frequent hijacks (Goleman 1995).

I've found that when we have already experienced multiple assaults to our psyche, our defenses are on the ready, become over-protective, and can trigger when the situation doesn't require it. This reaction makes performance management very difficult. In this defensive mindset, we can't digest feedback. If we can't process the feedback, we are unlikely to make the changes needed to improve our performance.

In fact, I have found that when we're insecure, we may not hear the feedback at all as we become completely focused on defending ourselves. Or we hear a distorted, less painful version of the words. It is as though our brain is selectively processing what will cause us the least amount of pain.

This next story illustrates that when an employee is defensive and quick to anger, this not only makes managing their performance difficult but can also be detrimental to the functioning of an entire team.

Emma, the sales manager for her company, was on a call with her fellow department managers to discuss recent challenges with a customer. She shared that the customer had told her they were unhappy with the progress the company's service team was making on their project.

Emma asked the group if the service team was having issues with the customer. Peter, the service leader, immediately hit the roof, swearing, and said he resented the implied accusation against his team, "especially from someone who didn't understand the service team's responsibilities"—that is, Emma.

He said that his team was already "working too hard for this customer" and that Emma didn't know what she was talking about.

Emma excused herself from the call, said that she was available later if Peter wanted to have a respectful discussion, and hung up.

This wasn't the first time in the past few months that Peter had acted out and sworn at colleagues. Peter's workload had become very heavy recently and the burden was making him insecure and defensive. However, instead of seeking help, he lashed out at everyone on the team. He was shutting down discussions, making it difficult to find any resolutions, and damaging relationships.

Emma didn't intend for her report of the customer's complaint to be a personal attack on Peter; his insecurity triggered his defensiveness because he perceived Emma's comments as a threat. An insecure person perceiving an interpersonal risk may lash out first to hurt the party they view as the threat before they themselves are hurt. In this case, Peter's defensive anger erupted as if Emma's words could mortally wound him. A situation that should have been about problem solving became a damaging conflict between two peers because Peter was hijacked by his emotions.

Although this conduct can be explained psychologically, it's unacceptable in the workplace. It can damage working relationships profoundly; those weakened relationships can impede efficiency and productivity, and thus corporate performance.

JUDGMENT OF OTHERS

The defensive, self-protective behaviors outlined in the past two chapters can reduce performance and frustrate those impacted by them. The behaviors are often construed as negative characteristics. However, they are defensive mechanisms triggered by insecurity, often subconsciously, so aren't necessarily a reflection of the true person.

Although the behaviors aren't a reflection of the real person, as the stories throughout the past two chapters have shown, the use of them can significantly impact the individual's performance.

In Chapter 3, Christine's sales numbers dropped when she lost focus as the result of Nicole's bullying, Company J's employees missed technological advancements because they were afraid of the reaction of the CEO if they made a mistake, and the launch of James's purchase order system was unsuccessful because he didn't seek buy-in from his peers.

In this chapter, we read how Lois used passive-aggressive behavior that confused and frustrated a more senior employee in her organization, Mark didn't meet the expectation that he would contribute positively to the corporate culture because of insecurity created by a bullying boss, and finally, Russell couldn't take constructive feedback and reacted negatively, which eventually resulted in him losing his job.

All of these situations resulted from people reacting negatively but self-protectively in response to their perceptions of danger in the environment or from individuals within it.

I've done the same. When I'm in a toxic environment, my natural ability to inspire and motivate seems to weaken, and my positivity becomes much harder to maintain. As a result, I've been perceived as aloof or unfriendly by those outside of my team.

Like Mark, I have the tendency to limit my contacts when I feel threatened. In a psychologically unsafe work environment, only the people on my teams or working directly with me get to know me. As a result, I have certainly lost out on connections that could have benefited both me and the business, and the positive impact I could have had on some cultures has been reduced.

Unfortunately, it's common that we jump to a negative conclusion when we don't like someone's conduct, rather than ask what is causing them to behave that way. When we jump to conclusions, we can miss seeing the true person behind the behavior, and the assessment can negatively impact working relationships.

None of the people in the stories started out as problem employees or poor performers, but they became that because of the threats in their environments. Unfortunately, due to their insecure states, they may end up believing that they are the problem. This can damage their confidence and impact their careers for the long term. Overall, this situation can cause employers to miss out on the skills of people who could make a difference in their businesses.

WHY THIS MATTERS TO YOU

Poor Working Relationships

Healthy, well-functioning relationships are critical in the development of high-performing teams and for efficient operations in general. When insecurity increases the prevalence of jealousy, passive-aggressive behavior, and defensiveness in the work environment, the quality of working relationships is in danger and likely to be suboptimal at best.

Toxic Corporate Culture

In a toxic work environment, many people will become insecure and turn inward to protect themselves from threats within the workplace. This will result in a disconnected workforce, where employees only interact with one another when necessary. The work environment will be low energy with an obvious sense of tension throughout.

Higher Risk of Bullying Behavior

When people are insecure, they may not have the confidence to stand up to or report bullies. This can allow toxic conduct to continue undetected in an organization and deteriorate the bullied employee's performance. The employee may leave the company if they don't see a route to report and escape the bully.

Poor Performance Management

Insecurity can trigger defensiveness, making it difficult for an employee to hear constructive feedback. Their reaction may be to deflect and make excuses rather than hear the painful words. If we don't hear feedback, we cannot do what's required to improve.

Inaccurate Judgment of Employee Performance and Potential

Leaders may not understand that an individual's performance is impeded by toxicity in the work environment. Employees with high potential may be passed over because of their declining performance that is caused by self-protective behaviors and not a reflection of their true potential.

CHAPTER 5

THE IMPACT OF A TOXIC WORKPLACE

"Insecurity is a social issue with psychological consequences, not a psychological issue with social consequences. In the workplace, the roots of insecurity are often found around us, not within us."

—Weber and Petriglieri

Society places significant importance on how we earn a living. This is fair since our jobs produce earnings that (for most people) determine the manner in which we live. But for many of us, our whole identity is caught up in what we do. I can't claim that I'm immune to that pull. For many years, being an executive was the cornerstone of my existence.

When we put this level of importance on our careers, it gives employers significant influence over our lives and thus over our sense of personal safety and security—our mental state.

However, our occupation isn't the only influence on us; we all have aspects of our personal lives that affect how we function at work. We enter the workplace with lessons already learned from our upbringings and adult lives as well.

Those experiences affect what we need from our employers. My tumultuous childhood gave me a high need for safety, and losing my partner reduced my tolerance for instability and insecurity for many years after his death. These experiences have impacted my choice of career and my choices of employers. These aren't negatives but simply realities. We all must find ways to navigate our worlds and balance the complexities of our lives.

As leaders, we cannot directly influence an employee's past or current personal life, but we can create a healthy workplace that doesn't threaten people's mental health by pushing their insecurity to an unmanageable level.

An employee will be better able to handle the challenges in their personal life if they aren't stressed because of negativity in their work life. The business will benefit from this because the dysfunctional behaviors outlined in Chapters 3 and 4 are less likely to be triggered.

To achieve a healthy work environment, leaders must be aware of and manage the factors in the workplace that lead to toxicity. This chapter discusses two of those factors: the environment and peers.

THE INFLUENCE OF THE WORK ENVIRONMENT

*"Psychological safety is a belief that one
will not be punished or humiliated for speaking up
with ideas, questions, concerns, or mistakes."*

—AMY C. EDMONDSON (2018)

Psychological Safety

When I decided to write this book, I shared my plan with a friend, who is a sought-after management consultant. I outlined my theory about the harm that insecurity can cause in the workplace. He responded, "You mean 'psychological safety.'"

This wasn't a term I'd heard before, so he explained. Without even realizing it, I had developed beliefs that dovetailed with a theory developed by Amy C. Edmondson and detailed in her book *The Fearless Organization*. Edmondson, the Novartis Professor of Leadership and Management at Harvard Business School, asserts that "psychological safety is a belief that one will not be punished or humiliated for speaking up with ideas, questions, concerns or mistakes." Professor Edmondson developed her theory through research into team behavior. My own views, acquired through years of experience in the corporate world, definitely align with her theory.

Edmondson's book discusses how knowledge and innovation will flourish in a psychologically safe environment because people feel safe to contribute their ideas. In contrast, people in a psychologically unsafe work environment harbor a real fear of punishment or humiliation when speaking up. The result is that innovation drops off and the gaining of knowledge is limited.

To state that a particular environment is psychologically unsafe gives the situation the weight it deserves, aligning it with the risks associated with a physically unsafe place. Feeling psychologically at risk will do temporary and possibly long-term damage to our mental health. Unlike physical dangers, we don't have to experience a direct injury to have an impact, nor does someone have to be close to us to do damage. Proximity isn't a requirement for psychological injury: a remote leader can be threatening and create insecurity as easily as a leader sitting right next to us can. Even the sense of potential harm from a threat to our mental state can reduce our focus and ability to do our jobs and in turn lower our contribution to corporate results.

Google conducted an internal study of 180 teams that showed how impactful psychological safety is. They found that *how* the teams worked together was more significant than the *composition* of the team itself. Teams that created a psychologically safe environment were more likely to use team members' ideas, and staff turnover was less likely within these groups. They also produced higher revenue for Google than those that didn't create safe environments, and executives rated them as more effective (Porath 2017). Higher revenue and lower staff turnover are strong arguments for the benefits of psychological safety.

A psychologically unsafe work environment doesn't just happen. It's the outcome of factors to be discussed in later chapters that impact our feelings of security at work. Among other influences, leaders or coworkers who are bullies, a lack of transparency, and unfair treatment can all contribute to an unsafe workplace.

If employees view the work environment as threatening, they won't be able to develop the trusting relationships needed to collaborate, innovate effectively, and establish security. An unsafe environment won't result in high performance or attract top talent. For these reasons, we must take heed and act to ensure safety in our workplaces, both physical and psychological.

Health and Safety Regulations Addressing Psychological Welfare

Employers have long been legally required to create "safe" workplaces. Governmental regulations around the world address both physical *and* mental safety. These mental safety regulations focus on discrimination, harassment, and bullying. Although it may not be explicitly stated in the regulations, the implicit goal of these legal obligations is the creation of a psychologically safe work environment.

The legal obligations typically require that organizations take steps, such as instituting policies and procedures for preventing discrimination, harassment, and bullying and creating the administrative procedures to support the submission and adjudication of complaints. Unfortunately, many businesses do only the bare minimum to meet these requirements.

Top leaders need to see a financial benefit to going beyond the minimum, and under-resourced HR teams don't have time to convince them. Many HR representatives are too busy putting out fires to be proactive.

As a result, policies and procedures are often boilerplate and saved on shared drives where they can be pointed to if there's an incident. These policies are rarely integrated into the corporate culture unlike similar guidelines around physical safety. Physical safety procedures are frequently audited and reviewed to ensure they are instilled in the culture. Imagine the cultural shift that would occur if leaders put equal emphasis on maintaining both physical and mental health in the workplace.

As it stands today, company efforts toward psychological safety typically include the requirement for all workers to sign policies and complete webinars or attend in-person sessions about discrimination, bullying, and harassment. Management can point to such efforts as proactive steps, should someone ever make a claim of mistreatment. However, employees sign the policies without reading them and speed through the courses simply to fulfill the obligation. They see these requirements mostly as a nuisance they have to suffer through (Chesnut 2020).

If an organization's policies or programs are designed purely to meet regulations and reduce liability, engagement and attention to them will be low because employees recognize them as an empty gesture. Liability mitigation won't ingrain the values in a culture or offer much protection to staff in an unsafe work environment.

To put some real numbers behind the impacts of psychologically unsafe workplaces, stress makes people three times as likely to leave their jobs, temporarily impairs strategic thinking, and dulls creative abilities. This can lead to burnout, which costs the United States more than $300 billion a year in absenteeism, employee turnover, diminished productivity, and medical, legal, and insurance costs (Peart 2019).

In addition, dealing with the repercussions of discrimination, harassment, and bullying, such as legal cases, terminations, and resignations, have real costs. This makes a psychologically unsafe work environment not only unethical but also time-consuming and costly. Companies should view the creation of a psychologically safe workplace not as a self-protective gambit but as good business.

Exclusion in the Workplace

Exclusion occurs when someone is left out of opportunities or events that they have a legitimate right or reason to participate in. There are different degrees of exclusion and they can be both intentional and unintentional. However, regardless of the intent, if individuals feel they've been unfairly excluded from a situation, their sense of safety in the related environment becomes reduced.

Exclusion is covered by employment discrimination regulations when someone is excluded based on a protected characteristic, such as gender, ethnic origin, or religion. This type of exclusion occurs in workplaces that are not welcoming of different backgrounds and lifestyles. In those environments, people are treated in a discriminatory and unequal fashion due to their diversity. These are grave offenses and should be taken seriously by organizations and reported when they occur.

Another form of exclusion is when someone is excluded in the workplace based on factors that are not protected by regulations. Although not illegal, these situations can create toxicity and work against the creation of a healthy corporate culture.

Employees can feel excluded from company plans if aspects of their personal situations aren't considered in those plans. For example, management may unthinkingly exclude some employees from participating in a social event if participation requires certain skills or abilities that they lack, such as playing a sport.

Exclusionary behavior at work can also be driven by self-protection. I've seen this behavior occur when employees are too fearful of the potential toxic conduct of others to include them in their projects or meetings, even when that person could have helpful insight. This was the case in the story in Chapter 3 where James excluded his peers from the decision on the purchase order system as he was too fearful of their hostile behaviors.

The story in Chapter 4 in which Heather failed to invite Lily to important meetings due to her jealousy of Lily's experience is an example of self-protective exclusion as well. In this case, Heather excluded Lily because her presence was threatening to Heather's mental state; Lily's success increased her feelings of self-doubt.

Some individual acts of exclusion can be subtle: a person may get left out of a series of seemingly small events or decisions, but the buildup of these situations can slowly deteriorate their sense of belonging. But the conduct can also be direct and obvious, such as ridiculing someone for their differences or shunning someone in social situations. Whether subtle or obvious, the person who is the target of the behavior can feel alienated from the group and their sense of safety in the environment will fade.

Exclusionary behavior can also take the form of a group of employees shunning a coworker or category of coworkers. This is often referred to as a clique. A clique is a group of people who have a common purpose or shared interest that spend time together and don't let others join their group. There can be a fine line between connected teams and exclusionary cliques. A connected team also has a common purpose or shared interest, but they don't function at the exclusion of others. They still welcome external opinions and participation. Connected teams can boost morale and engagement with their camaraderie. But if this team begins to exclude others, without a justifiable business reason, they can form a toxic, intimidating clique.

In one organization I observed, people who had worked there for many years formed a clique. They always sat together at company events, made a big show of their group lunches, and snubbed new staff or ignored them altogether. The top leader in this business had a tendency to play favorites; new people were viewed as threats to the longtime employees' relationships with the leader. The result was, this exclusionary conduct made it very difficult for new hires to integrate into the company and feel at home there.

I've also seen this behavior occur after acquisitions, when employees from the original company form a clique as a social barrier against the employees from the acquired organization or vice versa. This is a form of collective self-protection that can occur when there is significant uncertainty and change due to an acquisition. However, it can greatly reduce the success of initiatives to create a merged and connected culture.

The forming of cliques likely reminds you of high school. There, it's common for teenagers to form groups and shun those who don't align with their style or level of popularity. When adults use this same conduct in the workplace, it can cause feelings of insecurity in those who are excluded.

You may think that as adults we can ignore this behavior and not let it get to us. However, even if we're able to see the conduct as immature and that it's about the perpetrators, not us, it can still damage our sense of belonging within the organization and work against collaboration and productivity. It's not pleasant to be excluded, even if we understand the psychological explanation for it.

The Creation of a Work Persona

Exclusion can be extremely disruptive to a person's sense of security and self-worth. If an employee is being shunned on the basis of certain attributes or characteristics, they may feel shameful about those aspects of themselves.

If the employee perceives that not fitting into the social norms of the culture will exclude them from situations that are critical to their careers, they may feel compelled to conform and create a work persona: an identity created for work life that fits into what is perceived as acceptable. The number of people who feel the need to create this alternate workplace identity is high. A recent study (Smith and Yoshino 2019) found that 61 percent of employees cover some aspect of their true identities in their workplace.

I was one of these people; I created a work persona when I didn't have the same level of education as my peers and felt different due to my troubled past. I avoided talking about my history and myself in general for fear it would highlight this difference and lead to my exclusion. Creating and maintaining this persona can deplete the very energy that we need to grow our careers. Constantly thinking about what our work persona should do takes effort, as does remembering what the persona has said and done, because those things may not be our natural responses.

And in concealing our authentic selves, we're acknowledging, consciously or subconsciously, that an aspect of our real self isn't acceptable. This acknowledgment creates insecurity and will contribute to our "bucket of insecurity" becoming too full and triggering the behaviors outlined in Chapters 3 and 4.

The outcomes of exclusionary conduct are all harmful to the success of the business. Both the exclusionary behavior and the behaviors triggered in the excluded individual as a reaction to the experience are toxic to the work environment and detrimental to efforts to create psychological safety. The conduct will not only impact the target of the exclusion but also those who witness it and recognize the behavior as a sign of an unsafe workplace. It can impact the morale of a whole organization.

THE INFLUENCE OF COWORKERS

"'Insecure behavior' such as speaking less in meetings, or shying away from confrontation...is not the expression of a sensitive psyche. It is both a response to subtle threats and a way of fitting in."

—WEBER AND PETRIGLIERI

Although we go to work to earn a living, we also develop relationships there. Dysfunction within those relationships can impact us as deeply as dysfunction within our personal relationships.

In "Managing with the Brain in Mind," David Rock (2016) explains how the brain sees the work environment: "Although a job is often regarded as a purely economic transaction, in which people exchange their labor for financial compensation, the brain experiences the workplace first and foremost as a social system."

In my experience, this social system is thrown off kilter, triggering insecurity if unhealthy working relationships develop. Some of us may be able to ignore or rise above the toxic behavior of a peer, but for those of us with lower patience, higher sensitivity, or who are already dealing with challenging issues in our lives, the negativity created by the conduct may be more than we can bear.

In those situations, a toxic working relationship with a single individual can be enough to poison a workplace for someone, and they may seek a new job as a result. Cameron's story illustrates this.

Cameron enthusiastically joined Company G. She was excited about the team she would be working with, as her leader was highly respected and an expert in his field. He'd grown and sold multiple companies. Based on these successes, Cameron expected a stellar high-performing team to work with and learn from.

On her first day, she was shown to her office, which was right next to the cubicle of her boss's assistant, Danielle. Cameron introduced herself to Danielle and was greeted with a dismissive "Nice to meet you" as Danielle quickly turned back to her computer. Cameron figured she was busy, so she went on with learning her job.

In her next interaction with Danielle, she asked for help finding some documents. Danielle said, "You can't figure this out on your own? Don't you have a degree?" and rolled her eyes. This seemed like more than Danielle just being a busy person.

Unfortunately, this conduct continued. Every time Cameron asked for support or for Danielle to set a meeting with her boss, she would receive a snide comment and was treated like she was a major inconvenience. Cameron tried to ignore the behavior, but Danielle was the gatekeeper to her boss, so their interactions were continuous.

Cameron became anxious as the persistent hostility wore on her. She tried talking to Danielle. She said that it seemed they had gotten off on the wrong foot and she wanted to work together to build a great working relationship. Danielle said she didn't see a problem and that she wasn't there to be Cameron's friend.

After that, Cameron had little hope that the situation would improve without getting some help from higher up. Cameron raised the issue with her boss, but Danielle was savvy and had never exhibited toxic behaviors in front of the leader. To Cameron's

> dismay, her boss said he thought she was being too sensitive.
> Other employees had also raised the issue as they, too, had been
> on the receiving end of Danielle's toxic conduct, but the leader
> thought any talk of Danielle's negativity was jealousy because she
> was involved in his inner world.
>
> Spending every day in a tense environment wasn't sustainable
> for Cameron, so when a good job opportunity came up, she
> moved on.

Unfortunately, data has shown that toxic behavior like Danielle's is highly prevalent in work settings. A 2019 survey (Robinson 2019) found that 90 percent of respondents had directly experienced workplace bullying and 39 percent of those were bullied by a coworker, not a direct boss (Bortz n.d.).

If 90 percent of employees were physically injured by a coworker or boss, significant changes would be made. Emotional mistreatment needs the same level of attention.

Danielle's toxicity manifested in rude and shaming behavior. Another example of shaming is when coworkers insinuate in a meeting that a peer should have already known something when they ask a question: for example, the shamer may respond with, "Like I told you a week ago..." Shaming is a way to assert dominance, often by an insecure person feeling threatened. The action reduces the chance that anyone else will ask a question for fear they'll be called out, too.

Passive-aggressive behavior and team sabotage have also been identified as prime factors that create toxicity between coworkers (Kusy and Holloway 2009). Passive-aggressive behavior was discussed in Chapter 4; examples of team sabotage are being unprepared for team efforts, wasting time in meetings, and failing to share important information with peers.

Often, employees get away with toxic conduct because they are otherwise productive. Their behavior is justified as "quirky" or "well meaning." Coworkers are told to work around them and not get offended. In some cases, leaders don't want to take on the risks and challenges of replacing a problem employee, so they rationalize that everyone is overreacting. They may tell themselves it isn't that bad because the person isn't difficult with them.

However, as we saw with Danielle, many people are smart enough to be polite to the boss even though they aren't polite to anyone else. The boss could be so blind to or avoidant of the problem that they never even discuss the toxic behavior with the individual, regardless of the number of times the issue is raised.

Leaders need to recognize the reality that although an employee may produce and meet corporate objectives, the damage their toxic behavior does below the surface can be more costly. The performance of those on the receiving end of their conduct will suffer.

A study by Russell Johnson and colleagues at Michigan State University (2016) included data that workplace incivility has an average annual impact on companies of $14,000 per employee due to loss of productivity and work time. The researchers stated, "Being the victim of incivility leaves employees depleted because they must expend energy to understand why they were targeted and how to respond."

A different study found that once people are exposed to incivility, they're three times less likely to help others (Porath 2017). This will reduce the effectiveness of teamwork and collaboration in the workplace. In general, collaboration will be reduced by toxic conduct because people will avoid dealing with the person exhibiting the behavior. Whether we are able rise above someone's toxicity or not, we still won't enjoy working with them and will interact with them only when we absolutely have to. Great teamwork doesn't result when employees interact with each other only when there is no way around it.

As research shows, toxic behaviors often lead to dysfunctional work environments. However, there is a "chicken or egg" scenario here—that is, which one causes the other. I've found the prevalence of toxic conduct is higher in psychologically unsafe work environments. Employees seem to react to the perception of danger in the workplace self-protectively with their own toxic behaviors.

For this reason, before taking serious actions against toxic conduct, leaders must try to determine its root cause. There may be correctable aspects of the work environment triggering it.

Regardless of the cause of the behavior, it will negatively impact those bearing the brunt of it. The toxic conduct will increase the prevalence of insecurity throughout the organization and reduce the psychological safety of the workplace.

WHY THIS MATTERS TO YOU

Psychological Safety

In a psychologically unsafe environment, employees will be afraid to speak up and ask questions. This will reduce the innovation and growth within a company. In an unhealthy environment, staff turnover will be higher and productivity lower than in a psychologically safe workplace.

Employer Legal Obligations

A toxic work environment can put companies at risk of legal costs and damaged reputations due to bullying, harassment, or discrimination charges. Many organizations do only the bare minimum to meet legal requirements, which is not sufficient to ingrain positive values and behavior in a corporate culture.

Exclusionary Behaviors

The prevalence of exclusionary behaviors is higher in toxic environments. An employee who is the target of exclusionary conduct can feel alienated from their peers, which will increase their feelings of insecurity. An environment that accepts exclusionary behavior will have reduced collaboration and lower productivity.

The Influence of Coworkers

The quality of coworker relationships significantly influences employees' ability to maintain a healthy mindset about the workplace. Dysfunction within those relationships can greatly impact an employee's performance. Even a single toxic working relationship can be enough to poison a team environment and reduce the psychological safety of a work environment.

CHAPTER 6

STRATEGIES TO CREATE A PSYCHOLOGICALLY SAFE WORK ENVIRONMENT

We often hear about impressive perks used to contribute to positive corporate cultures at companies like Google. Healthy lunches, yoga classes, massages, and game rooms are some of the benefits touted in the media. Yet, many people will never work at companies of such scale and with so much money to invest in their work environments.

The majority of us will work in small-to-medium-sized businesses that yield lower profitability, so the return on investment (ROI) must be clear on all expenditures. It's not easy to calculate and thus defend ROI on purchases that enhance the workplace; the result may be lower investment in this area.

As a finance leader who helps companies decide where to spend their money, I understand this dilemma well. This chapter provides suggestions on how to create a psychologically safe work environment. Many of these recommended activities require the investment of intention and time but not dollars.

I'm a believer that the less tangible efforts I describe are actually more effective at creating a positive corporate culture than the obvious incentives listed above. A game room and free lunch may attract candidates to join an organization, but they don't guarantee a supportive safe work environment. That comes in an investment in how people are treated within a company. I strongly believe that the investment of energy is worthwhile to avoid the consequences of a toxic workplace.

Chapters 3 and 4 discussed these consequences. They range from those that are difficult to model, such as lower individual performance, to those that can be entered into a spreadsheet, for example, employee turnover. Even when the dollars cannot be cleanly laid out, if we look at the impact of insecure and toxic behaviors on the organization, the costs to the company associated with lost productivity, lack of innovation, and stunted growth are undeniable.

Companies can take many actions to create a psychologically safe workplace. There isn't a one-size-fits-all solution. Every business has its own pattern and balance of needs, depending on its stage, size, and culture, which must be considered to determine what is best for its teams and environment.

I ask that you consider the suggestions that follow in this and subsequent chapters and assess which are right for your business.

TONE FROM THE TOP

"In every team and every organization,
the responsibility for creating psychological safety
starts at the top. When people get penalized for voicing
problems and concerns, they learn that it's not safe
to speak up. It's up to those in power to open
the door—and keep it open."

—ADAM GRANT (@ADAMMGRANT, AUGUST 3, 2020)

No single action is a magic bullet to create a healthy corporate culture. However, one action is extremely valuable, and without it, no other actions will have a full effect: the head of the organization must authentically, explicitly, and publicly demonstrate that a psychologically safe and positive work environment is a top priority and critical to the success of the business.

I have found that if the top leader isn't a believer in the power of a healthy corporate culture, I can create a positive environment within my team's microculture, but my efforts to influence beyond my team are stunted.

In one case, I successfully created a productive, supportive culture within my finance team. Team members trusted one another and acted with respect and kindness. However, the organization's CEO had an aggressive leadership style and would raise his voice in anger and assert dominance to get his way. As a result, it often happened that employees external to my department would model the CEO, expressing their displeasure at the time to process an invoice or similar task by raising their voices to my staff and reprimanding them.

The CEO's conduct implicitly made aggressive behavior acceptable. I modeled healthy conduct and voiced my concerns to other leaders and the CEO, but this failed. When I realized that I couldn't create a consistently safe work environment for my team or myself, I left this company, and my whole team exited not long after I did.

Further validating the importance of senior leaders' roles in creating a principled culture, during certain regulatory audits, auditors assess whether a healthy "tone from the top" is exhibited by leaders. Leaders are powerful role models who establish the company's ethical climate. The integrity shown by these individuals is viewed as critically important for the creation of an ethical culture.

If you're the top leader in your organization, look at your conduct. Do you exhibit any of the dysfunctional behavior discussed so far? Do you create a psychologically safe environment? If not, think about what you can change.

If you're not the top leader and recognize that the head of your organization doesn't model healthy conduct, how can you support a change in this? Modeling the desired behaviors yourself is an essential step. From there, it depends on the relationship you have with the leader and your ability to influence them.

Although I will offer many suggestions to detoxify work environments, none of them will have their full effect unless the "tone from the top" is aligned with the goal of creating a healthy psychologically safe workplace.

ACCEPT AND EVEN CELEBRATE FAILURES, BAD IDEAS, AND MISTAKES

"Don't feel bad about your mistakes or those of others. Love them!"

—Ray Dalio

The sharing of new ideas and testing of innovative methods will sometimes end in mistakes or failure. To create a secure work environment for learning and growth, this fact of life must be welcomed. Learning from mistakes is an advantage that can set companies apart from their competitors. Businesses want to avoid situations like that of Company Z in Chapter 3, where shaming from the CEO made the team so afraid of making mistakes and taking risks that technological advancement stalled.

How can you create an environment where mistakes, failures, and bad ideas are an acceptable part of innovation, particularly when most of us have been brought up to believe mistakes are signs of weakness and bad ideas are shameful? In her research on psychological safety, Amy Edmondson (2011) has found that only leaders can build and maintain a culture that lets go of the "blame game" and allows people to be open about failures and learn from them. The "tone from the top" must model that mistakes are okay, and "Who did it?" will not be the main question asked whenever something goes wrong.

One method is for leaders to share their personal stories of failure or mistakes and the lessons they learned from them at town halls, in team meetings, and in one-to-one conversations with employees. They can also build stories of their mistakes and challenges into the company's history; for example, a founder's story could be frank about the failures that occurred before reaching success with the current business. These stories show that the failures were part of the ultimate achievement. This honesty will help to create an open culture that normalizes mistakes as part of the learning process.

Another approach is to celebrate employees who shared and/or tried novel ideas or methods, whether they were successful or not. The celebrations could include awards given at all-hands meetings where the award recipient discuss their idea or method, the process to discover/create it, and what was learned from the success or failure.

The goal of any approach you choose is to celebrate a willingness to try something new, uncover problems, and share innovative ideas, even if the idea fails or doesn't get implemented. The effort of generating ideas is in itself valuable. Even bad ideas can lead to brainstorming and the creation of great ideas.

Removing the stigma around failure and mistakes will reduce the fear of taking risks and increase the psychological safety in the environment. Employees will feel safe to try new methods and throw out ideas. Of course, this concept must be practiced within reason. All processes or ideas should be vetted and validated through appropriate procedures before they are implemented.

Few companies have a clear and formal process for evaluating and learning from mistakes. But Google does. And it isn't a process that requires big dollars to implement, so even small businesses can benefit from this method.

Google calls its official process for documenting and learning mistakes the postmortem. The practice involves three steps (Bariso 2018).

1. Identify the *most important* problems.

Since Google is a massive company and they don't want to waste time analyzing every little mistake, the first step is to ascertain whether the mistake was one of the most significant undesirable events among many. They do this by setting up criteria for that ranking. Every business will have a different threshold for the level and types of mistakes that would merit investigation.

2. Create a record.

In Google's words, "The next step is to work together to create a written record for what happened, why, its impact, how the issue was mitigated or resolved, and what we'll do to prevent the incident from recurring."

Asking specific questions helps:

- What went well?
- What didn't go well?
- Where did we get lucky?
- What can we do differently next time?

To answer them, include all involved in the issue.

This is the learning aspect of analyzing the error. A company will gain an understanding of how the mistake happened, how to prevent the error from happening again, and what's working in the business that prevented it from causing a bigger issue. The effort to sort all this out will save time down the road.

3. Promote growth, not blame.

Google acknowledges that this step is specifically intended to build trust that employees won't be punished for mistakes. Google says,

"Removing blame from a postmortem can enable team members to feel greater psychological safety to escalate issues without fear."

By implementing such a clear process for mistakes, instead of errors and problems being hidden away and creating shame, they will be brought out into the open where they can be learned from.

VALUE DIVERSITY AND PROMOTE AN INCLUSIVE ENVIRONMENT

The most successful and innovative company I've ever worked at welcomed extroverts *and* introverts, all hair colors, tattoos, liberals *and* conservatives, morning people *and* afternoon people. We could all be ourselves; as a result, we truly knew one another and enjoyed strong, productive working relationships. The connections were authentic because few facades blocked collaboration and little insecurity limited social interaction.

Companies that create environments where employees feel comfortable showing their true selves—through their style, culture, opinions, and ideas—have loyal and secure staff. We learn from people who have taken different paths to success than ours and from people who have different backgrounds and lifestyles.

Despite these benefits, expectations that employees conform to the norms of a culture aren't rare in the business world. The 2019 Deloitte study that found that 61 percent of employees covered some aspect of their true identity at work also reported that 50 percent of those same employees said their leader's expectation that they hide a part of themselves led to a reduction in their commitment to the organization.

To ensure an expectation isn't created (intentionally or not) that to be accepted on a team, people must conform to an implicit cultural norm, management should evaluate its hiring and advancement processes for biases and ensure an inclusive corporate culture. Creating environments where diversity is celebrated will benefit everyone.

Diversity in Hiring

We've all felt the natural attraction to things that we can relate to. We can't help but look closely at people who went to the same university, grew up in the same town, or got experience at a company we're familiar with. It piques our interest. During the hiring process, leaders need to resist this tendency and look for talent and experience beyond the people who are familiar.

A basic approach I've had success with is to clearly define, in writing, the needs of the role that I'm recruiting for. (I'll provide a high-level description of this process in Chapter 10.)

Outlining the attributes and experience required to succeed in a position will focus attention on those needs. The hiring manager won't be as easily distracted by the less significant factors that would otherwise bias them. They can also assess and compare all candidates against these needs. This comparison will reduce the risk of bias toward someone's background resulting in overlooking their actual shortcomings compared to other candidates, or a lack of familiarity with someone's history resulting in their disqualification even though they have all the required competencies.

In short, we must ensure that we don't eliminate qualified candidates because we don't recognize ourselves in them. Through this, we will increase the diversity in our hires and therefore in our organization.

Promoting Inclusion

Ensuring the recruitment of a diverse group of employees is necessary for creating an inclusive environment. However, it's not sufficient: leaders must ensure that once selected candidates have joined the team, they're not excluded from internal activities for their differences.

Some questions to consider in the assessment of an organization's level of inclusivity are:

- Do the company's core values include a statement on the importance of diversity and/or inclusion?
- Does the company have a diversity, inclusion, and nondiscrimination policy and a procedure to manage incidents of exclusion?
- Has the company held diversity or inclusion training sessions?
- Are the needs of all employees considered in event decisions or is everyone expected to conform to the needs of the majority?
- Do leaders know what makes each member of their teams unique?

If the answer to many of these questions is no, it's time for leaders to take steps to ensure inclusivity is promoted and valued in their organization.

In addition to enacting policies and procedures and holding training sessions, leaders can model the value of inclusivity by learning about their teams and allowing employees to share who they really are. This can be done in one-to-one discussions or broadly through efforts like ice-breaker games where people can learn about each other. These efforts will be most effective if leaders share something unique about themselves first. This sets the tone for everyone to share what makes them different.

These initiatives should always be optional as some individuals prefer not to share personal details at work. However, those who do want a sense of community and belonging in their workplace will prosper in an environment that provides the opportunity for it.

One leader that I spoke with had an excellent suggestion for breaking the ice and promoting inclusivity.

> Company W asked each new hire to make a list of five interesting things about themselves to send to all employees as an ice breaker when they joined the organization.
>
> When you have to list five things about yourself, it has to be more than the school you attended and your last job. Something unique was learned about the person.
>
> This ice breaker was done by every team member, from leaders to part-time service reps. It provided an excellent introduction of new people. It also created a reason to approach one another authentically. Employees could ask about a fact on the list or share that they had the same hobby. Conversations were prompted with something personal, which set an excellent tone for workplace relationships going forward.

Initiating this type of engagement and implementing the elements from the questions above set the tone that diversity is respected and each employee is valued for their uniqueness. However, beyond setting the tone, it's also critical that leaders clearly state there is zero tolerance for any type of exclusionary conduct in the organization.

Given the subtleness of exclusionary behavior, companies should periodically remind employees, through training and corporate communications, of the conduct that can be exclusionary. And the top leader should model inclusive behavior to ensure the importance of it to the business is clear.

As such, they must avoid falling into an exclusionary clique themselves, such as going for lunch only with other executives or sitting with the same group at every social event. Top leaders should make efforts to greet all employees when they see them and to learn about those in lower levels of the company. These actions sound basic, but they matter. They demonstrate to all staff that they are important.

These steps will increase the sense of safety and belonging in the work environment and allow for greater collaboration. The prevalence of protective behaviors will drop.

MODERNIZE THE
HUMAN RESOURCES FUNCTION

*"The HR model at many companies—
particularly established ones that have been in
business for a long time—is increasingly outdated and
insufficient to help them navigate the current environment.
HR still functions in its traditional role as a service
provider that focuses on transactions, rather than
as a true partner to the business units."*

—Reinhard Messenböck et al.

The profile of Human Resources (HR) departments has evolved significantly over the past twenty years. We have seen different terms coined for the department, such as People and Performance, and more HR leaders included at the executive table. Yet, not all companies have moved with the times. There are still largely two schools of thought about HR in the corporate world.

The Old-School Version of HR

An older view of HR's role sees it as administrative and transactional, with a priority on protecting the business against legal claims. In that world, HR has a limited role in developing leaders and tends to be viewed warily by employees who see them as a protector of the company, not a supporter of the people. HR mainly executes agreements, processes workforce changes, and ensures all of the t's are crossed and i's dotted. It isn't fully empowered to impact the culture.

In my experience, when HR only fulfills the old-school role, there's a greater chance of toxicity in the work environment and lower psychological safety. This is exemplified in a scenario I witnessed. An administrative employee was assigned the responsibility for HR. The administrator didn't have any experience or education in HR so only knew how to perform the transactional aspects of the role.

They were also closely aligned with the CEO, to whom they provided administrative assistance. This connection magnified the perception that HR was only there to protect the company and not the staff. As a result, none of the employees would go to HR for support since there was a lack of trust. There were many toxic individuals in this organization, but no action was taken. Bullying and exclusionary behavior were rampant. However, with no one to report them to, no route to change existed.

Through this experience, I saw that if HR isn't empowered to act beyond an administrative role, there's no one to advocate for the employees and educate leaders on the benefits of a healthy culture. As a result, it's more likely a toxic work environment can occur and remain.

The New-School Version of HR

Alternatively, in the progressive view of HR, businesses are empowering HR specialists to fulfill those responsibilities but also to be strategic partners to all leaders. They are critical players, advocates, and advisors in the creation of healthy cultures and high-performing teams.

The Benefits of a Progressive HR Function

An Advocate for Employees

If HR is empowered as an advocate, the department can provide a communication forum for staff that is separate from their leader. Ideally, all employees have a healthy direct manager who supports them, but failing that, HR can be the backstop.

For example, if a worker feels threatened by their manager, it's difficult for a subordinate to go to their boss's leader, so HR represents a safe middle ground. In the absence of a trusted HR person to speak to, a toxic situation could continue, and the organization might lose a valuable team member who feels that their only option is to leave.

Support Leaders with Performance Management

The modern HR department is a key resource in establishing systems for performance assessment, rewards, and accountability. When

HR is properly resourced, it's able to have regular contacts with leaders to support performance management and identify team challenges or toxic conduct in the workplace.

An employee may be meeting their technical job requirements but not the interpersonal requirements; an experienced HR professional is equipped to support leadership to establish an explicit, documented plan for the employee's expected behavioral change that includes predefined consequences if the change is not forthcoming. A knowledgeable HR team member is an essential management resource that can provide sophisticated guidance, assist with diagnosing the root cause of toxic conduct, and proposing corrective actions to halt the spread of toxicity throughout the organization.

Promote Healthy Workplace Behaviors

As discussed in Chapter 5, most companies at best only meet the workplace safety requirements related to discrimination, harassment, and bullying. This is largely due to insufficient HR resources. All HR professionals want to ensure that employees are aware of what constitutes mistreatment and make it clear that their businesses don't accept this. If the HR department is sufficiently resourced, the team can meet the day-to-day needs of the organization while also taking proactive measures to support a psychologically safe work environment.

Develop the Workforce through Strategies for Learning and Growth

Employee development and succession planning are critical for the long-term success of businesses; however, it's an area of effort that often slips down low on the priority list since other in-the-moment tasks always seem to take precedent. A strategic HR professional will have this task as an objective and will work with leaders to ensure they consider the development of their teams. This will increase the number of employees who are prepared for senior roles and succession when required.

Demonstrate That a Safe Workplace Is Valued

Empowering the role of HR in the establishment and protection of a healthy culture signals to the workforce that top leaders value a positive environment. The implication is that employees themselves are valued. By virtue of the action to fund and empower HR, employees will feel safer.

Awareness of Market and Industry Compensation Trends

Without an HR resource focused on compensation and benefits trends, an organization can easily get left behind as competitors evolve and target their most valued employees. An HR professional will monitor the job market to reduce the risk of losing staff simply because their managers aren't aware of the high demand for a skillset and fail to progress salaries and benefits at the pace of the market. This also ensures that fairness in compensation is maintained, which is otherwise a cause of insecurity that will be discussed in Chapter 9.

Creating a Progressive HR Voice

My focus on the need for a strong HR representative is not meant to say that leaders in the organization may not see the value in a healthy corporate culture. However, if cultivating that culture is not clearly part of someone's job description or tied to their performance objectives, competing goals and deadlines may dilute effort in that particular direction. An empowered strategic HR leader will ensure that the health of the corporate culture stays on the priority list.

The level of HR resources needed for a business will depend on its size, needs, and organizational complexity. This requirement is also impacted by factors such as geographic dispersion, the competitive nature of necessary skills, the rate of employee turnover, and the experience of company leaders.

Small businesses may not have the financial resources or team size to support a dedicated HR person, but this doesn't mean there isn't a need for those skills and perspective.

If a company doesn't have the size or resources to hire a dedicated full-time HR person, I suggest recruiting a fractional or part-time HR professional or consultant or empowering a senior leader in the organization who has the interest and desire to take specific responsibility for the culture.

If a non-HR leader is empowered to take on the responsibility, ideally they would have a broad understanding of all departments' needs. If the selected person hasn't already, they should take courses or attend workshops to educate them on human resources and the creation and impact of psychologically safe work environments. This person should ensure that the health of the corporate culture stays at the forefront in all decision making.

The key point is that even if the organization isn't at the size where it merits or can support a dedicated HR professional, someone is still at the leadership table whose job it is to ensure that impacts on the workforce and the corporate culture are considered in all decisions.

PROCESS TO ADDRESS HARMFUL
BEHAVIORS

Even our most emotionally balanced employees can have something occur in their personal lives that has them unconsciously exhibiting destructive behaviors that reduce the sense of safety in the work environment for their coworkers. June, in this next story, is an example of this.

> June, a project manager at her firm, was having trouble controlling her anger. This had led to outbursts at two employees in separate events. Each of those individuals had been so upset by the display of anger that they had reported it to the company's HR manager, Alan. They both said that not only had June raised her voice, but she had been physically aggressive. In one case, June had vented her frustration at the employee who also felt that June had moved inappropriately and intimidatingly close to her. In the second case, June had been frustrated with a customer, not the employee. Nevertheless, she had raised her voice in a way that made the employee uncomfortable and slammed her hand against the wall. In both cases, the affected individual was concerned about the lack of control that June exhibited.
>
> Both Alan and June's direct manager, Susan, were surprised by the reports. June had worked for the business for three years and was a high performer; she had never exhibited this type of conduct before.

How would you handle this situation?

It's challenging when a historically great employee suddenly exhibits troubling behaviors. No matter the positivity of an organization's culture, incidents in which employees display conduct that's harmful to their coworkers or doesn't align with the company's values will occur.

Despite management's best efforts to screen and assess candidates, bad hiring decisions do happen and a candidate whose behavior ultimately doesn't align with the company's values may join the team. However, the employee in question may also be someone who's had an abrupt change in their personal situation that has overloaded their ability to cope with workplace demands.

I'm an example of someone whose conduct shifted unexpectedly. When I lost my partner, I closed in to protect my psyche. I was no longer the connected leader I had previously been. This wasn't destructive, but it was certainly confusing and disruptive to the regular cadence of my work and team. My employer at the time didn't have a well-funded empowered HR team to identify the issue, but I self-identified and resigned from my role, sensing that in my state of grief, I was no longer the best person for the job nor able to handle the work environment any longer.

Many personal situations can disrupt our mental balance to the point that it affects our behavior at work. For example, if someone is dealing with an illness that causes chronic pain or is managing family problems such as divorce or child-rearing issues, the stress can make them impatient and short-tempered. Even something as common as prolonged sleep disruption can make someone irritable and quick to lose their temper.

Regardless of the cause of the conduct, companies should have a procedure in place so it's clear what actions should be taken to investigate the situation and support the employee if appropriate, while ensuring the behaviors don't continue and negatively impact coworkers and the culture.

An established process to address harmful behavior in the workplace is essential for many reasons:

- The process acts as a deterrent to harmful conduct since clear consequences are in place.
- Inaction by leaders to address harmful behavior can be taken as acceptance of it, encouraging such conduct to spread throughout the company.
- If inaction causes employees to conclude that harmful behaviors that don't align with the expressed corporate values are accepted within the organization, the significance of those values will plummet.

The longer that destructive conduct continues in an organization, the greater the consequences will be on working relationships and the overall culture. People are likely to forgive a one-time negative interaction with a peer. However, if multiple instances occur, it becomes less likely the relationship can be repaired.

The behaviors can be addressed promptly when there's clarity on the steps to take because a formal process has been established. This process should take into account the severity of the harm the conduct caused; certain steps may not be appropriate depending on the extent and impact of the behavior.

These are specific recommended elements to the process:

- The process must provide employees with a clear route for reporting conduct that is counter to the company's values or safety guidelines. The process should also state that there is zero tolerance for these behaviors and that there will be no repercussions to employees who make a report.

- To ensure fairness to all involved, an investigation must be undertaken to confirm the validity of the report.

- The investigation should include an initial discussion with the employee exhibiting the behavior to inform them that an issue with their conduct has been reported. If the employee is exhibiting the behavior, they may not be aware of it, or they are aware of the conduct but not of its harmful impact, so this step gives them an opportunity to make adjustments.

- If the behavior is proven to have occurred, an effort should be made to understand the root cause of the conduct and if appropriate, whether support is needed. There may be an underlying reason for the behavior which, if addressed, could solve the issue.

- If it's within a leader's power to do so, support should be considered to help the employee manage any challenges that may be causing the behavior. Options include adjustments to workload, schedule, or location.

- If applicable, the employee should be reminded of services available under the company's benefits plan.

- The employee must be informed of the consequences if their behavior isn't modified and that their conduct will be monitored.

- After the initial intervention, the employee's behavior should be observed to determine whether there are any further recurrences.

- If the conduct does recur, then additional actions must be taken, such as the preparation of a behavior improvement plan. The plan must clearly communicate that if the employee doesn't follow the plan and improve, it can result in termination.

To be clear, **this process and behavioral standards must also apply to the conduct of leaders, even at the highest level.** Research has shown that few actions halt harmful leadership behavior other than applying a zero-tolerance policy (McClean et al. 2021). I will specifically discuss the impact that toxic leadership behaviors have on organizations in Chapter 12.

Back to the situation with June. Her company did have a policy to address harmful conduct. The policy was clear that behavior that doesn't align with the organization's values must be reported to HR or the person's superior. The employees had followed the policy in reporting the incidents to Alan.

Alan sat down with June and started the conversation by telling her that her contribution to the business's success was valued. However, concerns had been raised about changes in her conduct. Tears immediately began to well up in June's eyes.

She said, "I knew that's what this was about...I'm so sorry. My son recently went through a scary incident—he was attacked by a dog—and now, he's afraid of everything and isn't sleeping well; he shows up in my room in the middle of the night, terrified and looking for comfort. I'm not getting nearly enough sleep, and I'm worried about him. I have no patience, and my fuse is short."

Because June opened up and recognized the issues with her behavior, it allowed the discussion to move to how the company could support her.

June then shared, "I'm finding my workload difficult, given

the situation at home, so if anything goes wrong, I break." Alan suggested that they discuss her workload with Susan.

He asked if there's anything else that could improve the situation. June said that she needed help controlling her emotions and asked if the company would sponsor her to learn coping skills through an anger management class; this would give her tools to manage her temper. Alan agreed to this, and June registered for a class the following week. Meanwhile, Susan moved one of June's projects to another manager to lighten her load until she got through this challenging time.

Alan checked in with June two weeks later. June shared, "My sleep is still affected, but I feel so much calmer now, knowing that my employer is supporting me. The course gave me great tools to use when I feel my temper rising. And the reduction in my workload has helped considerably."

There were no further reports of angry outbursts from June.

ESTABLISH A MENTAL HEALTH COMMITTEE

Despite a low physical safety risk in some work environments, such as offices, corporate health and safety committees have long been commonplace there. The reality is that office environments bear much greater risk to employees' mental health than they do to their physical health. And we cannot forget that stress can lead to physical symptoms as well.

The stress of heavy workloads, toxic working relationships, and unexpected changes, among other factors, can significantly impact an employee's mental and physical well-being. To address this risk, leaders should consider creating a mental health committee or at a minimum, adding psychological safety to the mandate of an existing health and safety committee.

The mission of a mental health committee should be to increase awareness and education about mental health issues in the workplace, to remove the stigma around them, and to provide resources to those in need. It should also act to ensure that mental health is considered in operational processes and interactions and during times of change or crisis.

It's important to ensure diverse representation so the committee has advocates who speak for the specific needs and concerns of its overall workforce. Although senior leadership, and specifically an HR representative, should be at the table, the decisions, ideas, and actions should be developed by the group.

To be most effective, the committee should have a high-profile champion within the business who is passionate about the committee's mission and can advocate for it authentically. Ideally, this is the CEO or president; if not, it must be a senior leader within the organization or worksite.

The creation of the committee validates the importance of mental health as essential to the wellness of employees and the company overall. This validation can open up space for staff and their leaders to discuss mental health issues and can result in greater support for those dealing with related concerns. The direct effects of the committee are a reduction of employee absenteeism and turnover, lower health-related costs, and an increased sense of support and care from the employer. This sense of support will increase the psychological safety of the work environment and employees will have a greater willingness to share their challenges with their leaders.

Tone from the Top

An organization's ability to build a psychologically safe work environment will be limited unless the top leader believes in and advocates for it. Employees look to leaders for the behaviors that are acceptable within the workplace. This makes it critically important that leaders exhibit conduct that aligns with the company's values and supports a healthy, safe workplace.

Accept Failure and Mistakes

Innovation requires mistakes and failures that can be learned from. If employees feel safe to try out new ideas and processes that may result in mistakes or failures, companies will benefit from the resulting innovations. They will support the progress and growth of the business.

Diversity and Inclusion

Businesses that create environments where diversity is celebrated will benefit from greater perspectives, ideas, and unique approaches from their employees. They will also have a more secure and committed workforce.

Human Resources

Company leaders will have greater success in the creation of healthy cultures and high-performing teams if they partner with skilled HR professionals. A strong and empowered HR leader will ensure a healthy work environment remains a strategic objective and will support all employees to reach their full potential.

Process to Address Harmful Behaviors

A clear process to address harmful behaviors in the workplace ensures employees know what action to take when harmful behavior occurs. The action of reporting the conduct will stop it when it does happen and the existence of the process will reduce the prevalence of the behavior since consequences are clear.

Mental Health Committee

Mental health is a common workplace issue that impacts employee performance. A mental health committee can ensure mental health issues are considered in corporate initiatives and during crisis situations. The existence of the committee also reduces the stigma around the topic.

CHAPTER 7

THE IMPACT
OF UNCERTAINTY

*"All of life is uncertain; it is the perception
of too much uncertainty that undercuts focus and
performance. When perceived uncertainty
gets out of hand, people panic and
make bad decisions."*

—David Rock

Certainty is a human need, one that is so significant that our minds tend to see uncertainty at some level as a threat. Our brains protect us from the threat by preventing us from focusing on anything else until certainty is achieved (Carter 2020). Clearly, being unable to focus on anything other than a perceived threat will reduce productivity toward work objectives. An obvious implication of this is that a business in which employees are in a constant state of uncertainty is not good for the bottom line.

I observed earlier that each of us has a maximum threshold for insecurity; I believe the same is true for uncertainty. Each of our thresholds are different, but if the uncertainty goes above our personal tolerance level, we become anxious and insecure.

Uncertainty within our work environment and uncertainty in our personal lives can combine to affect our productivity on the job. I was functioning quite well in a startup environment despite its instability until my partner suddenly passed away. The challenges at the company had been within my tolerance level, but once my partner was gone, the heightened ambiguity in my personal life made the uncertainty and difficulties in my work life unmanageable for me. I had to leave that company and seek a workplace with greater stability and fewer tensions.

As leaders, we can't control what's happening in an employee's personal life that may impact their tolerance for uncertainty. However, we can control factors in the work environment that create uncertainty and contribute to the overall insecurity that the employee must contend with. One of these factors is the safety of an employee's job.

JOB INSECURITY

Job insecurity is a belief that our job is at risk or that a critical aspect of it, such as location, boss, salary, or responsibilities, is going to change (possibly for the worse). A lack of certainty about the safety of our job contributes to the overall levels of general insecurity that we feel.

Employees tend to look to the company's leaders to remove the uncertainty around the safety of their job—to answer, "Is the business financially stable?" "Am I meeting expectations?" "Do I fit into the plans of the business?" Providing our staff with honest, clear information about our organization's current state, its plans for the future, and what each employee's roles will be in those plans is key. The cadence of this communication depends on the pace of change within the organization but should be delivered on a consistent basis and when circumstances evolve.

Situations will occur, such as a significant downturn in the economy, in which job insecurity is simply the reality and beyond the control of the business. I've experienced the challenge of a poor economy twice in my career, first during the financial crisis in 2008 and again during the COVID-19 pandemic. During both, society was deeply impacted by the negative economic news in the media. Job losses were extensive; those who still had their jobs were often uncertain about how long they'd have them. Anxiety was pervasive. We'll discuss crisis situations further in the next section and methods to reduce insecurity in the face of crises in Chapter 8.

However, an employee's sense that their job isn't secure may not always reflect the true situation. I've had many discussions with people who were utterly convinced at some point in their career that they were going to lose their job, when the reality was that they were highly valued and secure in their positions.

Their incorrect judgment of the safety of their job may be the result of external influences, such as general anxiety due to factors in their personal life or the impact of negative news reports. But it can also be due to internal company influences such as unclear organizational goals, vague individual performance objectives, and/or a general lack of transparency on the part of the company's leaders. In these cases of poor communication, the employee is left to rely on what they *suspect* their boss thinks of them or what they *think* is happening in the business. Lack of clear information, filtered through a negative bias, can lead the employee to imagine and believe the worst possible outcome is nigh for their job or their organization.

Whether the perception of job insecurity is correct or not, it can still contribute to toxicity in the work environment, because the defensive behaviors outlined in Chapters 3 and 4 can be triggered. The following sections describe common factors that can contribute to the perception of job insecurity and that will increase feelings of insecurity in general.

LACK OF TRANSPARENCY

> *"A lack of transparency*
> *results in distrust and a deep*
> *sense of insecurity."*
>
> —The Dalai Lama

Transparency refers to the willingness of whoever is in control to honestly share why and how something that's affecting others is being done. Employment is a situation in which people have limited control over the security of their position; an absence of transparency by leadership can provoke anxiety and insecurity.

Like certainty, human beings crave transparency because it's central to creating certainty. Given our desire for it, if we don't have transparency about a situation, we tend to come up with our own version of what's happening and why it's happening. We attempt to create certainty for ourselves.

Brian J. Brim (2016), a Senior Practice Consultant for Gallup, explains the outcome of poor transparency: "Very often, partial information leads people to fill in the blanks with the worst-case scenario. This can lead to more instability, insecurity and disengagement."

It's a significant danger to businesses if employees assume the worst-case scenario whenever transparency is lacking. A lot of otherwise productive energy can be wasted worrying about outcomes that may never occur.

Transparency during Crises

Transparency is particularly vital in times of crisis, when uncertainty is at an exceptionally high level. A leader can ease the anxiety created by crisis situations with transparent, timely communication, but they can also compound the stress of the situations by providing insufficient information.

If leaders fail to communicate the possible impact of a crisis on their business and their strategy to mitigate any negative effects, staff may question the leaders' ability to manage the crisis and protect their jobs. Absent transparency, employees may look elsewhere for answers and reach incorrect and often dire conclusions. These conclusions may drive them to look for new jobs. Or they may take action themselves to establish certainty and create comfort.

The COVID-19 pandemic crisis created significant uncertainty. Some companies acted quickly to address risks and communicate their plans to staff, which reassured them that leaders were on top of the situation. But other organizations took too long to declare their strategies to manage the risks, which only magnified the uncertainty their employees already felt.

In some instances that I learned of, during the early days of the pandemic, leaders delayed communicating any action plan in response to the crisis because they felt the potential impacts of the situation were unclear. However, they also failed to share that they were actively monitoring developments and considering alternative actions. The information vacuum forced their employees to make decisions for themselves to address their personal risk.

For example, some businesses delayed closing their offices. Employees were still expected to come in to work. For those who had no alternative to get to their workplace other than public transit, this increased their risk of exposure to the virus.

Those employees were put in the untenable position of having to choose whether to work from home without the approval of their boss or continue their commute, risking exposure and suffering enormous anxiety. The stress created around making this decision was inevitably damaging to productivity.

In this situation, transparency and timely communication could have eased employees' concerns and saved hours of lost work. The need for transparency applies to any crisis situation. If staff aren't informed by their employer of the effect of the crisis on the company and steps being taken to mitigate those effects, uncertainty and insecurity will increase, along with self-protective behaviors.

Transparency in Times of Change

Times of change also require high transparency. This applies whether a change could be considered good or bad by employees, because even seemingly positive changes can create uncertainty and insecurity if the details aren't clearly communicated and understood.

To demonstrate this, let's say you have two choices to drive to an important destination:

1) Take a new route that goes down an unknown road.
   You can't see what is along this road or at the end.
2) Stick to a tried-and-tested route.

Someone whom you don't know well is telling you that the new route is faster, but they haven't given you any evidence to support that it is. On the other hand, you're certain that your regular path will get you to your destination.

Which option would you choose?

Most of us will pick the known and familiar route. Why would we willingly change to a different path if we're uncertain what's at the end or what will happen along the way, especially since reaching the destination is important?

We would only change our route if we trusted the person telling us that option 1 was faster or the outcome was guaranteed. Given the uncertainty created by the new option, we may even resist and procrastinate about moving forward at all.

This same outcome can happen at work. If leaders are implementing a new process or system but simply communicate that it will be more efficient and fail to provide evidence or an explanation of exactly why the change is occurring, employees are likely to resist and stick with the old reliable method. They will see no reason to give up the security of the old way.

In my experience, there's often a fear of giving up "old ways" that have always worked for us. In general, we have an inherent bias toward maintaining the status quo (Blount and Carroll 2017) and opting for the safe, known method. But this resistance will be magnified if there's uncertainty around the reason for and impact of the change, or if we don't trust the person leading us down the new path.

Therefore, transparency and trust are vital to reducing insecurity and increasing buy-in around changes. Yet, we tend to misjudge the impact that the uncertainty surrounding changes can have on employees and the level of communication needed to ease anxiety around them.

In fact, a 2019 survey found that only 36 percent of employees felt that employers were honest with them about changes that would occur in their company's last workplace transformation (*2019 Edelman Trust Barometer*). The survey result is concerning since a workforce's support is critical in all business transformations and this support will be lacking if trust is low.

A business transformation in which a lack of transparency is far too common is corporate acquisitions. I've gone through six acquisitions and have witnessed the negative impacts poor communication about the purchase can have on employees.

New people and strategies are introduced, which creates many unknowns. Leaders need to make focused efforts to be transparent and build trust with employees on both sides of the transaction. Otherwise, in the face of unknowns and increased insecurity, staff will focus on what they *don't* know rather than what they *do* know, reducing their attention on doing their jobs while, without sufficient information, they try to make sense of the changes in their altered environment.

Even when a leadership team thinks they're being transparent by openly stating decisions, it may not be sufficient to create certainty for employees. Many people will not take comfort from a decision if they don't understand the logic and reasoning behind it, particularly if they see factors that don't support the conclusion.

Here's a perfect example. Where I work, a potential change in office locations is always at the top of the list of employees' post-acquisition worries. Most of my career has been spent in Vancouver, Canada, an expensive city with high commercial property costs and salaries compared to many jurisdictions with similar talent pools. It's therefore logical to assume that any organization that acquires a business based in Vancouver would consider moving the office to a lower-cost location or integrating the acquired company's team into the offices of the acquirer, which is usually located elsewhere.

The approach I saw many acquirers take was to simply state that they weren't going to move the office, end of story. The acquirers honestly believed that this simple statement would be sufficient information to satisfy the staff of the acquired company. It wasn't.

Those employees, who were already dealing with the general uncertainty that acquisitions create, were well aware of the cost issue and all the logical arguments to move the office. A simple "we won't close the office" wasn't enough proof to calm their insecurities, and it failed to establish trust.

Without a clear understanding of the decision process behind the assurance that the company was remaining in Vancouver, employees didn't feel comfortable that their jobs were truly safe. In fact, they suspected that information was being withheld from them. As a result, productivity dropped as they spent valuable time talking about and fearing a move. Whenever a new person was hired at another location or someone was let go from the Vancouver office, the staff speculated that it was all part of the "master plan" to close the office.

I've seen uncertainty around office locations go on for years after acquisition because issues were never properly addressed.

True transparency includes explaining the why. If the reasons for a decision aren't clear, it can be difficult for our minds to settle and consider it as the truth. This results in distracted employees who spend time trying to figure out the why themselves. If staff believe there are multiple issues about which they aren't being fully informed, they may conclude they can't trust their leaders overall and they will be suspicious of every message those leaders deliver.

Given this, why do communications about changes so often miss the mark? There are a number of factors:

- **Underestimation of the awareness of potential or intended changes.** Leaders often don't consider how obvious the signs are that changes are coming. We may attempt to be discreet about meetings or hide documents or files related to a change. However, people are observant, and walls are thin. News typically seeps out and employees know something is happening before leaders expect they will. Uncertainty around what's happening can create distrust and will make it harder for changes to be accepted when they are announced.

- **Reluctance to share too much too early.** Leaders may want to wait until they're absolutely certain of an outcome before sharing it with their teams. However, as noted above, employees will notice signs of potential changes. Without clarity, they'll often assume the worst of the signs and make assumptions that can distract them when the change is eventually communicated.

- **Providing insufficient time to prepare for and mentally process change.** Delaying the communication of a change can leave employees insufficient time to process the information and prepare (including mentally) for changes to their work environment.

- **Overestimation of employees' level of acceptance of the change.** Last, leaders have often been discussing and deciding on a change for some time prior to announcing it to their teams. Leaders may have already mentally moved on to acceptance of the situation so they don't grasp that employees haven't digested the same amount of information. As a result, insufficient details are provided about the change or the reason for it. This reduces the workforce's comfort around the situation and, in turn, their buy-in of it.

All of these factors will increase the risk that change initiatives will fail or not reach expectations and will diminish employee's trust in their leader and their sense of security.

UNCLEAR BUSINESS STRATEGY, GOALS, AND OBJECTIVES

We feel safest about the future when we think we have insight into what it will bring. When we've picked a life partner, a career, bought ourselves a home, all those things give us certainty. We have a plan. This same principle applies to the organizations we work for.

The Invisible Corporate Strategy

If there is a lack of clarity about the business's strategy, its employees will find it hard to feel secure about their future there. If the company's apparent lack of direction persists for an extended period, it can drain motivation and reduce employees' ability to contribute to the achievement of corporate objectives (Blount and Leinwand 2019).

Think about yourself when you're out for a Sunday walk with no clear plan versus when you're walking to meet a great friend. When walking to meet your friend, your pace will be fast and determined. You know where you're going and what the payoff is at the end. Without the known payoff, you may walk slowly and aimlessly as you look at the sights around you, uncertain of where to go next.

Far too many people feel they are walking aimlessly through their workday. One study found that only 40 percent of employees say they're well informed about their company's strategic objectives (Peart 2019). This is an area where many leadership teams seem to fail.

Among the potential reasons for the absence of clear communication of strategy and purpose is that the founder or CEO has a clear direction for the company in their head but fail to share it with the wider team. This may be an unintentional lack of transparency if they genuinely think the direction is clear to everyone because it's clear to them.

Or sometimes, in an entrepreneurial company, the direction can actually be fluid, changing in response to market demands as the founder takes opportunities and shifts strategies as they see fit. If an employee chooses to work for an entrepreneurial startup, they may be prepared for instability and be excited by it, as some of us truly are. However, if they aren't, the lack of clarity around the direction of the business will create insecurity.

Both scenarios, and others that limit transparency around a company's future, can create uncertainty for employees.

Undefined or Unrealistic Individual Goals

The company's high-level direction is critical, but employees also need certainty around the direction of their own role. I've found that my own sense of safety and motivation in my position decreases when my job feels purely reactive rather than working toward a clear end goal.

In one of my past jobs, the business didn't have a clear strategic direction, and as a result, individual goals were ill-defined and lacked purpose. My coworkers and I were constantly having to adjust our tasks depending on the current burning issue, which sometimes changed day to day. If we weren't rushing to put out a fire, there was uncertainty over what we should do next since the priorities weren't clear. Deadlines drove us to get work done, but motivation between those deadlines was low since we weren't clear on what we were supposed to be working toward next.

If employees aren't certain of their contribution to the success of the business or the expectations of their roles, they're unlikely to reach their full potential due to the uncertainty and insecurity the lack of direction creates.

However, goals also need to be set with caution. It will only create further uncertainty if goals are unclear or unachievable. This next story of Company M highlights how unrealistic and ever-changing goals can create job insecurity.

Company M was only in its second year of operations and hadn't created a stable process to set business objectives and individual goals. The company's leadership team had the habit of setting unachievable objectives in one month and then moving the target date the next month.

In the beginning, the unrealistic goals created insecurity because employees didn't know how they would ever achieve them. Some people froze in their uncertainty of how to accomplish their assigned tasks. Others sped ahead, trying to get work done as quickly as possible. Both often failed to meet their objectives, either due to paralysis or because their speed caused poor-quality results.

However, as the ever-changing goal setting persisted, it became almost comical, and employees stopped taking the targets seriously, which removed any motivation they could have provided. Although coworkers joked among themselves about leadership's lack of foresight, they began to feel uneasy about what this meant for their future.

They weren't feeling the sense of accomplishment that comes from achieving a goal and also weren't sure if their jobs were safe. Those who had in-demand skills began listening to the offers when recruiters called, and employee turnover increased.

It takes time and focus to develop an accurate strategy and reasonable deadlines, particularly in fast-moving industries. But Company M's story shows the harm that can be done if the process isn't fine-tuned.

Continually resetting goals because they were unrealistic causes anxiety due to the original difficulty of the goal and is compounded by the stress of an ever-moving target. This unnecessary pressure diminishes trust in leadership.

It's good business to adjust a strategy that isn't working, but if goals are reset every month, the process should be reviewed and adjusted, or the company risks losing employees who see the lack of stability as a bad sign for their future with the organization.

Lack of Feedback on Performance

"Evaluate accurately, not kindly.
In the end, accuracy and kindness
are the same thing."

—RAY DALIO

Clear goals are a critical factor in establishing job security. However, to maintain an employee's confidence in the safety of their position, ongoing communication is needed about their efforts toward meeting those targets and fulfilling the other requirements of their role.

Rick's story shows the impact when performance issues aren't communicated in a timely manner.

Rick had been in his role for four months. Although at a high level, he thought he'd mastered most of his assigned tasks and reached his defined goals, he couldn't shake an underlying feeling that he wasn't meeting expectations. Yet his boss hadn't said anything to him about his performance.

He finally asked his manager, Sasha, if he was doing okay, and she responded, "Yes, it's fine," but didn't provide any real input. Sasha was a junior leader who wasn't experienced in performance management. She was uncomfortable giving negative feedback.

Rick sensed something was being left unsaid. The lack of input on his performance was making him nervous that his job wasn't secure. He started making mistakes as his focus was blocked by his anxiety. Sasha noticed Rick's errors and fixed them but still gave no feedback or mentoring.

At the six-month mark, Rick had a performance review with Sasha, where she couldn't avoid having a full conversation. She finally came out with her criticism, and it validated all of Rick's anxieties. Many of the tasks he'd thought he'd been doing correctly he was actually doing wrong—and he'd been doing them wrong for months.

Sasha put him on a performance improvement plan. Rick had become so insecure from the uncertainty and anxiety leading up to the review that he wasn't able to meet the requirements of the plan and was let go.

Like Sasha, many people don't like to give input unless it's positive. Sometimes a lack of experience in performance management creates discomfort, but often leaders avoid providing negative feedback because they don't want to harm their relationships with employees.

I, too, have had concerns about the impact of constructive feedback on my rapport with my team members. I like to lift people up, so giving input that may upset someone isn't something I look forward to. But I've gotten my head around it by realizing that withholding feedback actually isn't kind at all. We aren't supporting someone if we don't give them information that will help them improve. In the story, Rick may have been able to correct his performance if he'd known what he was doing wrong, but instead he became insecure.

People often sense when there's an issue with their performance or when something is unsaid by their leader. This will cause uncertainty and decrease their confidence. As Rick did, the employee will become anxious as they feel they aren't living up to expectations but don't know why.

Keeping silent on performance issues could cause someone to lose sleep as they worry about their job, what they may be doing wrong, and wonder when they will be pulled aside and spoken to. This anxiety will further deteriorate their performance even lower than it may already be.

Continuous Layoffs and Terminations

"Do everything you can to avoid layoffs.
They don't just hurt the people you lose—they crush
the morale of those you keep. Survivor guilt
and fear are real costs."

—ADAM GRANT (@ADAMMGRANT, MAY 13, 2020)

The timing and need for layoffs and terminations are difficult to predict; often, business requirements change quickly. However, to avoid the situation in this next story, it's in the best interest of employees and a healthy corporate culture to have a clear workforce plan, so layoffs don't regularly occur.

Company Y was undergoing significant post-acquisition restructuring that involved both layoffs and recruiting. Unfortunately, due to the addition of new decision makers and an evolving strategy, staffing decisions were constantly changing.

Positions were frequently added and old ones removed. Sometimes the people in the "no longer needed" roles could be moved to other positions, but many were laid off.

Leadership felt that competitive pressures in their market created a short window in which to succeed. As a result, layoffs for poor performance were also frequent. Employees were given very little time to improve; once given feedback, if they didn't turn their performance around quickly, they were let go. The continuous stream of terminations created a toxic work environment.

Every other week, someone was being walked out, and often, no announcement was made about their departure. New faces appeared in the offices weekly with little fanfare. A distrust of management was created. Employees became nervous every time they saw HR enter their area of the office. They didn't want to be noticed or risk doing anything that would put them on the chopping block. The level of insecurity was sky-high.

Predictably, instead of focusing on their work, the employees spent their time gossiping about the latest change and wondering who would be next. Fearful for their jobs, they withheld information that they felt may put them in the line of fire. This meant problems were hidden and bad news was buried.

The CEO ultimately didn't receive the information needed to make proper decisions. This contributed to a poor strategy, missed deadlines, and cash flow problems which eventually led to the demise of the business.

We humans are resilient creatures, so if one of our team members is let go, we'll be bothered for a period of time, but we'll recover and refocus on our work. However, if we hear of continuous layoffs, this will create a bigger distraction with concerns about whether we could be next.

Feelings of job insecurity can have a greater detrimental effect on employees than actual termination itself (Dekker and Schaufeli 1995). I've seen this firsthand with people in extreme states of anxiety, wondering if their job was at risk. If they were laid off, it was a relief rather than continuing with the uncertainty, fear, and torment of wondering.

Apart from creating a sense of job insecurity for those who remain in the business, frequent layoffs have these effects on the organization:

* Each time a termination occurs, routines are disrupted. Anytime we remove a position from the workflow, it impacts all those who interacted with that role. This can reduce efficiency for a time and create stress for the employees who must figure out how to adapt to the change.
* Productivity will be reduced. Apart from the inefficiencies of changing processes and training new hires, unless there's sufficient transparency around the departure of the employee, those left behind will spend time worrying about their job and trying to figure out who may be next.
* If employees don't understand the reason for the exits, morale can deteriorate as employees are disheartened by peers being let go.
* Distrust in management will be inevitable if the employees don't understand the reason for the layoffs or think their exited peers were treated unfairly.

In addition to these impacts, if a company gains a reputation for constant terminations, it will harm their recruitment efforts. Given a choice of joining an organization with a stable environment versus one that has a reputation for constant layoffs, most will choose the former.

Having said all of this, I do recognize that the reality is that although terminations can be reduced with accurate workforce planning and strong recruiting practices, employee exits will still sometimes be required due to poor fit or performance, restructuring, or financial challenges.

When they are required, transparency around the communication is critical, and if possible, layoffs should be done all at one time, rather than creating a stream of constant departures that employees' psyches cannot recover from. Transparency around the communication of layoffs will be discussed in Chapter 9.

WHY THIS MATTERS TO YOU

Certainty Is a Human Need

If employees are uncertain about aspects of their job or their employer, they will find it difficult to focus until certainty is achieved. This will reduce their productivity and, in turn, the performance of the business.

Lack of Transparency

Like certainty, humans crave transparency. The uncertainty created by low transparency can lead to insecurity and disengagement. Transparency is particularly critical in times of change or crises. In those situations, leaders can calm employees' fears with transparency, or they can exacerbate them by leaving staff uncertain of the business's strategy in the face of the change or crisis.

Unclear Company Purpose and Objectives

Creating certainty requires clarity on the organization's direction and the plan to get there. If this clarity isn't provided, it will reduce employee's motivation and create insecurity.

Lack of Communication about Performance

Lack of communication about work performance can create self-doubt and anxiety for an employee, since they don't know how they're doing. Whether a staff member is reaching expectations or not, uncertainty around their performance can distract them and lower their productivity.

Continuous Layoffs and Terminations

A culture of continuous layoffs creates distrust in management and job insecurity throughout the business. This will decrease motivation and productivity. A company's reputation can also be damaged by frequent layoffs, which can impact their ability to find quality candidates in the future.

CHAPTER 8

STRATEGIES TO REDUCE WORKPLACE UNCERTAINTY

In business, as in the rest of life, there is no true certainty. None-theless, leaders *can* provide their staff with confidence that their company has a sustainable business model, a clear path to reaching its objectives, and that each employee has a role in the future of the organization.

This chapter provides recommendations on the type and quality of information that should be provided to employees to give them this confidence. With it, they will be more engaged and focused in their jobs, undistracted by worrying about the future of the business and whether they might be safer elsewhere.

ESTABLISH AN AUTHENTIC
COMPANY IDENTITY

When we think about what a company stands for, our minds usually go to the outward customer-facing brand it projects to reach its target market. To build a successful workforce, a business needs to communicate its corporate identity internally to its current and potential employees as well.

The foundation of a company's identity is its vision, mission, and values. These elements are the basis for the development of trust and security in the employee-employer relationship.

Articulate a Clear Vision and Mission

Chapter 7 established that when employees have a sense of certainty about their organization's direction and their roles in reaching the desired destination, they'll have greater motivation to dedicate their full effort. A *Harvard Business Review* survey further validates this in its finding that over 90 percent of companies with a well-defined purpose deliver growth and profits at or above the industry average (Blount and Leinwand 2019). I believe that the secure workforce that results from this clarity of purpose is a significant contributor to those strong corporate results.

Yet, Gallup research shows that only 22 percent of employees strongly agree that leaders in their organization have a clear direction for the business (Brown and Robison 2020). Evidently, many leaders haven't recognized the need, and the opportunity, to do better in defining the desired future state of their organization. Doing so is worth the investment of resources since after all, how can employees support their company's long-term objective if they don't understand what it is?

Vision and mission statements are the most common tools used to communicate a business's purpose, both to employees and to external stakeholders. There is often confusion between the two. A *vision* is the desired future state for the organization. It's aspirational but still achievable. A *mission* is more concrete and focuses on the state that the organization is working toward in the present, whom they're working for, what they're aiming to achieve, and how they're working to reach the intended state.

Here are Toyota USA's vision and mission statements from its website, illustrating how they differ:

Vision: To be the most successful and respected car company in America.

Mission: To attract and attain customers with high-value products and services and the most satisfying ownership experience in America.

Toyota USA's vision is aspirational as they aren't there yet; there's a lot of competition, but the goal is achievable in the long run. The mission is concrete; the customer is the who, Toyota cars are the what, and providing the most satisfying ownership experience is the how. Toyota's workers can understand and embrace these messages.

A company's leadership team can craft the vision and mission statements on their own. However, if the budget allows it, the engagement of a strategy consultant can be helpful to assist with defining the purpose and putting it into meaningful statements.

Once the mission and vision are established, the progress toward them should be regularly communicated to employees in the interest of maintaining their motivation and sense of security. How "regular" is defined will depend on the business's momentum: a high-growth company may require quarterly updates, while annual updates may be sufficient for a mature, lower-growth business.

The vision and mission must evolve with the strategy. If management makes a strategic shift, the statements must be revised to ensure that the sense of certainty provided by these statements isn't undermined by the disconnect between words and actions.

Establish Corporate Values and Live Them

The vision and mission are the desired destination, whereas an organization's core values statement tells all stakeholders what the business stands for: what's ethically important to the company, what considerations and criteria the company's leaders will factor into their decisions, and how stakeholders can expect to be treated by those within the company.

Examples of common themes for core values are *integrity*, *diversity*, *loyalty*, and *transparency*. If an organization sets transparency as one of its values, stakeholders will expect that when decisions are made and changes occur, they will be fully informed about them. People who appreciate transparency will gravitate toward this business because it has this value.

If someone's decision to accept a position with an organization was influenced by their alignment with the corporate values, they will quickly become disheartened and insecure if upon joining, they discover their leaders and peers don't act within that values system. To maintain their trust as well as the integrity of the values statement, the values must be embodied within the corporate culture. Ideally, a core team of employees (including some leaders) who hold the values the company wants to live by should develop the statements.

The established values should become the cornerstones of how the business makes decisions. As discussed in Chapter 6 under "Tone from the Top," the organization's leaders must consistently demonstrate the corporate values if the employees are to do likewise. The values should be integrated across all people practices, including recruitment, onboarding of new staff, and performance reviews. This integration will ensure the values become part of the way of life at the company, with continuous reminders of their importance.

Having meaningful corporate values will create common ground to connect those in the workforce and create comfort in the belief that all actions by leaders will be taken in alignment with the values. Maintaining consistent adherence to the values contributes to a healthy, functional culture.

An example of well-defined corporate values is the "10 Core Values" at Zappos, an American online shoe and clothing retailer:

1) Deliver WOW through Service
2) Embrace and Drive Change
3) Create Fun and a Little Weirdness
4) Be Adventurous, Creative, and Open-Minded
5) Pursue Growth and Learning
6) Build Open and Honest Relationships with Communication
7) Build a Positive Team and Family Spirit
8) Do More with Less
9) Be Passionate and Determined
10) Be Humble

All Zappos workers take an Oath of Employment, committing to these values (Zappos, n.d.).

The Zappos 10 Core Values communicate that this organization prioritizes serving the customer, focuses on growth and learning, cares about its people, and knows openness is the right way to get clear results. They also convey that it's important for the company to do all of this while being financially responsible.

How do their values make you feel? If Zappos truly walks this talk, it's a place where I would absolutely want to work.

ENSURE THAT COMPANY OBJECTIVES AND INDIVIDUAL GOALS ARE ACHIEVABLE AND ALIGNED

As outlined in Chapter 7, goals and objectives are key to maintaining a sense of job security. A company's objectives should paint a clear path to the achievement of its mission. Individual performance goals should be defined in alignment with those objectives.

This alignment assures employees that the company has a plan to achieve its mission. They will see that the leaders' words and the planned actions are consistent. Both perceptions encourage trust and reduce insecurity.

However, depending on the size of the organization and the level of a role within it, the connection between an employee's individual goals and the company's ultimate objective may not be direct. For example, if the business's mission is to create the highest quality product in their industry, the goals of those within support departments such as Finance may not be directly connected to the plans for the product. Yet, I believe there is still merit to establishing how every employee's role is essential to the achievement of the company's mission.

The connection may be as simple as highlighting to an Accounts Payable (AP) team that vendor relationships are extremely important in reaching the corporate objectives. Vendors provide essential components for the product. Therefore, the AP team's goals of ensuring accurate vendor payment processing and building strong vendor relationships are critical. This alignment gives value to what can be considered a mundane task but is vital in all businesses.

If leaders make this effort to demonstrate how individual goals connect to the overall mission of the organization, it will increase each employee's job security and motivation. The exercise validates that every role matters and contributes to the success of the business.

The goal-setting process at Company L in this next story exhibits this principle.

Company L's leaders met with each of their employees annually to establish individual goals for the year. These meetings included a review of the company's mission and vision and the strategic objectives toward achieving them. During the review, the leader would highlight how individual goals supported the achievement of the overall mission.

Goals were clear and attainable with reasonable timelines and measurable criteria to determine success. Bonuses were tied to the achievement of the goals. The alignment of desired results to the bonus payout provided a clear outcome and additional motivation for reaching the targets.

Goals were reviewed on a quarterly basis to ensure progress was being made. This was also an opportunity to assess whether any changes during the quarter had affected the relevance or achievability of the goals. If adjustments to the goals were required, they were formally made at this time.

The feedback from Company L's employees was that the process showed them where they fit in the organization and how

> they contributed to the success of the business. They knew their purpose and were motivated to achieve it.

In addition to establishing each employee's connection to the corporate mission, Company L also ensured that the individual performance goals were clear, achievable, reasonable, and measurable.

A common methodology to achieve this clarity is the use of SMART goals. SMART stands for specific, measurable, attainable, realistic, and timely. Using the SMART criteria ensures employees have certainty over the critical aspects of their expected performance. They know the details of each goal, how they will be measured, when they must be completed, and that they are achievable.

A useful test of whether SMART goals have been set successfully is if an outsider to the process could understand the requirements to achieve the goal and what success looks like. I once had a leader set a goal for me to be "more aggressive"—certainly not something that was either specific or easily measured.

I like the SMART approach because it creates clarity and certainty for the employee. However, an element of flexibility is also required in goal setting.

Despite the importance of certainty, companies can't be locked into strategies that over time may not bring the desired outcome. As new information comes to light, leaders must have the ability to adapt and fine-tune. The workforce has to be doing the right things to support the changed strategy effectively, so their goals have to be modifiable as well.

An additional benefit of flexibility is that when leaders show they are aware of and adapting to a changing business environment, the employees will feel more secure. If changes are well-communicated to staff, they will take comfort if they see their employer is aware of the need to address issues in their environment and modify their plans.

The COVID-19 pandemic crisis is an example of a time when objectives had to be quickly adjusted. Many companies had to change their operations and strategies, for example, accelerating remote access or switching to delivery from in-store service.

This required the reprioritization of both corporate objectives and individual goals. Those companies who took control and made changes quickly demonstrated to their workforce that they could handle the situation. This provided some relief and reduced uncertainty for employees during a period of unprecedented upheaval and widespread, profound insecurity.

When goals and objectives must be adjusted, this should be done formally; those that are replaced should be explicitly marked as no longer operative. It may seem obvious that the old goals and objectives are implicitly irrelevant going forward. In actuality, I have seen people persist in completing goals because they think they must in order to receive a positive performance review or ensure their annual bonus. Complete clarity avoids wasted effort and ensures that the employee doesn't feel misled.

However, the adjustment of goals should take place due to the unforeseen need to change direction rather than as a result of ineffective goal setting or overly ambitious expectations. We saw the impact that unrealistic and ever-moving targets had on the team at Company M in the last chapter: staff began to look for jobs elsewhere due to the deterioration of their confidence in management.

Leaders sometimes choose to use ambitious "stretch goals" to deliberately challenge their teams. A stretch goal is a target that is set above what is expected to be accomplished and is used to motivate employees to reach exceptional results. They can be useful to encourage high performance. However, leaders need to be careful about setting excessively bold individual goals as they can create fear.

Before setting stretch goals, we should ensure they aren't so bold that they are unreasonable. We must also consider the employee's mental state. If there has been a lot of change or recent negativity in the environment, this may not be the time for goals that are extremely challenging. Or at a minimum, we should build confidence-boosting, easier-win goals into the strategy to increase security and motivation toward attempting the aspirational tasks.

MAKE ONGOING
PERFORMANCE DISCUSSIONS
A CULTURAL NORM

"°ne of the greatest shortcomings of traditional performance management systems is a lack of ongoing feedback and coaching."

—Gallup

Along with setting and monitoring the achievement of specific individual goals, leaders must also manage and provide feedback on general performance. If employees know they're meeting all performance expectations or are being supported to make improvements, they will have more confidence that their job is safe.

Questions are often raised about what effective performance management entails today. Are annual performance reviews a thing of the past? How do we manage performance in today's often-remote environment? How do we give employees the flexibility and autonomy they want while still managing their work?

The above are all valid questions, and the answers depend on many factors, including the seniority of the individual and the nature of the job they are performing. I don't believe a universal approach to performance management exists. However, in any approach, certain elements must be considered to ensure an atmosphere of psychological safety and to minimize insecurities.

The following story of Nina and Steve demonstrates many of those elements.

> Nina, the marketing director at her company, had built a supportive relationship with her marketing manager, Steve, starting the day he joined her team. She told him then that she saw his potential and that she thought he would surpass her in the organization one day. Nina truly meant that.
>
> Steve had the education, commitment, and drive to have an extremely successful career. The only thing holding him back was his lack of confidence. This issue caused him to look to others for guidance too often rather than trusting his own judgment. He also tried to do things too quickly in an effort to be efficient, and it sometimes led to sloppiness, despite his strong skillset.
>
> Nina had regular one-to-one sessions with Steve in which they often discussed his performance. As a natural part of their meetings, it never became a taboo topic. In one such discussion, Nina asked Steve what he thought he needed to do to improve, and Steve said, increase his self-confidence and slow down the pace of his work to improve his accuracy.

> With Nina's openness about her belief in Steve's potential,
> she'd created an environment where he felt safe acknowledging
> his challenges. He knew Nina's goal was to support him. Because of
> this openness, they were able to develop an approach to empower
> Steve to improve his problem areas.

The critical aspects in establishing an environment where healthy performance management discussions can occur are developing a strong leader-employee relationship, providing ongoing and timely feedback, and avoiding negative and personal commentary.

Establish and Maintain a Secure Leader-Employee Relationship

Productive performance discussions require a firm foundation of trust. Without trust, the employee may approach the conversations with apprehension or outright fear.

Nina's creation of a healthy relationship with Steve is exemplary. An employee must believe, as Steve did, that their leader wants to support their growth and success. Then, if necessary, constructive negative feedback can be delivered effectively since there's an understanding that its purpose is to improve performance in furtherance of the individual's professional growth *and* company objectives.

If a leader is viewed as a threat, the employee's defense mechanisms will be activated. We saw this in Chapter 4 when Jake tried to give Russell feedback about his tardiness. The feedback triggered Russell's fight-or-flight response, rendering the delivery of the message ineffective.

I will discuss specific strategies to develop secure leader-employee relationships in Chapter 13.

Provide Ongoing and
Timely Performance Feedback

Nina had set the tone through her one-to-ones with Steve that talking about performance would be a normal part of work life. As a result, their performance discussions became second nature and weren't threatening to Steve.

Apart from reducing the threat of performance discussions, making them a normal part of the process has additional benefits:

* Developing a practice of ongoing feedback enables communication on specific performance issues in a timely manner. This avoids the situation noted in Chapter 7 in which Rick sensed dissatisfaction with his performance and, not having the opportunity to learn whether something was in fact wrong or how to correct it, became increasingly anxious. His work suffered while his manager waited until a formal performance review to provide feedback.
* Timely feedback is effective because the situation at issue is recent. The employee can remember the specifics of what occurred, making it easier for them to adjust their work or behavior.
* Immediate feedback ensures that the situation doesn't persist uncorrected until the time of a formal performance review. Delaying the discussion can allow the problematic condition to become habitual.

Avoid Negative or Personal Commentary

Constructive feedback can be difficult to take at the best times, but the challenge will be magnified if the feedback includes unnecessarily negative and/or personal commentary.

Some individuals may need the consequences of their actions or behavior repeatedly highlighted if they don't seem to understand the impact, but such people are in the minority. If an employee is well aware of the effect a mistake had on their team or the company and clearly feels bad about it, their leader restating or expanding on that negative impact isn't constructive. It will only fill the employee with shame and insecurity and doesn't tell them what to do differently. In my experience, most people are hard enough on themselves so don't need the negative impacts of their behavior or mistake belabored.

An example of unnecessarily personal commentary is the use of an accusatory tone: "You made a mistake," "You should have known better," "You screwed up." The focus should be on the mistake and how to correct it, not on the person who made it. Someone who knows that they've made a mistake will come into a discussion about it feeling insecure; the conversation will be more effective if the leader gives constructive feedback in a nonthreatening way, without personal accusations that would trigger a defensive reaction. The feedback should be factual and presented as something that can be worked on together to improve, rather than a situation that the employee alone has to figure out.

I had a leader who delivered constructive feedback exactly in this manner. In that company, I simply had too much to do, and the result was that some tasks were slipping through the cracks.

My boss approached me to discuss the issue, but instead of raising it as a condition that was my fault, he said that he knew I was being faced with a tough workload and asked what we could do together to make it better.

He came to the discussion with solutions, proposing task management tools. The discussion didn't make me defensive because there was recognition that I was doing my best in a tough situation. The problem-solving approach to improving my performance was truly collaborative. The safety of the discussion allowed me to be objective about how I could enhance my performance rather than becoming defensive.

Improved performance benefits both the employee and the company. A wise organization will train leaders at all levels in the skills to engage in this type of open and safe dialogue with their direct reports.

CREATE TRANSPARENCY

Achieving the right tone and appropriate balance of information in corporate communications is imperative and challenging. Such messaging has been made both easier and harder by the evolution of technology. We can connect more efficiently and faster now, but we also need to decide between the many channels available for our messages.

Despite all the methods of communication available to us and our shared innate desire for transparency, the fact is that many of us aren't naturally great communicators. Lack of experience and insecurities can work against our ability to connect with others and can limit the sharing of important information.

A 2017 Gallup poll found that only 13 percent of employees strongly agreed that the leadership of their organization communicates effectively (*State of the American Workplace*). This result could be easily improved with some thoughtful, consistent actions. This section shares strategies to improve internal corporate communication and achieve the level of transparency needed to avoid the creation of insecurities.

The right starting point to determine what effective communication with employees should look like is talking with them. Ask them how do they feel about the current level of communication? How much communication would they like? What would they like to hear more about? How would they like to receive those messages? These discussions will provide useful information to determine the level of communication needed, but I will also highlight some aspects to consider.

Consider the Frequency and Method of the Message Delivery

Important messages need to be repeated many times to ensure they sink in. Use a variety of channels to communicate—for example, live meetings, email, bulletin boards, and text messages. This ensures the critical points reach the target audience through their preferred communication method; individuals vary in their information-processing requirements—some do best with auditory input, others with visual. In practice, this means that some employees may find reading long newsletters challenging and prefer live meetings to digest information, while others may prefer reading messages to fully process them. The goal is to ensure that information is received and understood so employees don't feel blindsided by later events or changes.

Speak the Truth, Ensure Alignment between Words, Actions, and the Reality of the Situation

Communicating messages in a timely manner in a format that can be understood and retained is half the battle; what the message says matters, too. Words need to align with reality because mixed messages create uncertainty and can breed insecurity and even suspicion.

A company I worked for regularly held town halls at which only successes were touted by leaders; no mention was made of the fact that the business was losing money and had failed to meet critical objectives. The employees saw very clearly what was happening; the messages only created distrust. The takeaway lesson from those meetings was that employees couldn't believe the words of leaders.

Communication requires a balance between inspiring a workforce and giving a realistic picture. I have concluded that to influence and build respect and trust, leaders must always speak the truth, even if that truth isn't good news.

Share the Reasoning behind Management Decisions

When significant decisions are made, the reasoning should be shared with the employees, to the extent that privacy considerations and the preservation of competitive secrets allow. This openness not only creates clarity but also preserves trust and will increase buy-in.

In the office location example in Chapter 7, employees of the acquired Vancouver businesses were deeply skeptical and distrustful in response to the acquirers' professed commitment to stay in the city. They clearly saw the objective financial reasons to move their offices to a new location. If the companies genuinely saw the value in keeping the location, a better approach would have been to share the cost-benefit or other analysis that was considered in arriving at that conclusion.

Having an understanding of the inputs to the decision-making process will increase employees' sense of security, and they will trust their jobs are safe, so long as the factors in the assessment don't change.

Whenever it's reasonable to do so, involve employees in the decision process. The company will gain the benefit of diverse insights while easing the general level of anxiety.

Provide an Avenue for Follow-up Questions and Create a Feedback Loop

People continue to ponder announcements after first receiving the information; they will think of questions that didn't come to mind immediately. Additionally, distractions can arise even while important messages are being delivered. It's therefore valuable to create a route for posing questions after the fact, such as an email of a contact person, and a process for ensuring questions are answered and that responses of general interest to all employees are shared.

A feedback loop within this system is helpful to ensure continuing communication between leaders and employees on critical issues. An example of a feedback loop is a system in which, after an initial communication by top leaders, department heads raise the topic in their meetings with their teams to clarify and provide an opportunity for questions. Another is the creation of champions for an announced initiative who speak to individuals throughout the organization to ensure that the initiative is understood.

These are methods for general communication. Next, I share an approach that I have seen used effectively to communicate on a topic that has particular weight for employees: layoffs and terminations.

Communicating Layoffs and Terminations

As discussed in Chapter 7, the communication of terminations and layoffs is often mishandled. Because the negative impact of this can be so great, it's important to offer some guidance on how to convey this news effectively. Here's the story of Ryan, a leader who handled a termination well.

> Ryan hadn't yet been in the role of CEO for sixty days, but it was already evident to him that the director of customer service, Marshall, didn't have the skills needed for his role. When Ryan first joined the company, he was told that Marshall had been having performance issues for months already. Ryan observed Marshall's performance and saw that the problems were real and significant. Ryan discussed them with Marshall.
>
> Unfortunately, even after multiple conversations about his performance and offers of support, Marshall continued to make mistakes, which were costing the business credibility with its customers, as well as money.
>
> Ryan was aware that a leader firing someone shortly after joining the team can create insecurity for others in the organization. But for the good of the business, he had to make the decision. Ryan let Marshall go.
>
> Ryan was intentional in his communication of Marshall's exit. He held a meeting with all of Marshall's former direct reports and

the customer service team members. He explained that he and Marshall had discussed the needs of the director role and had agreed that Marshall didn't have the right skillset for the company at this time. This message had been discussed with and agreed to by Marshall.

Ryan assured the team there were no plans for future layoffs and that everyone's job was secure if they fulfilled their roles. He didn't say there wouldn't ever be other terminations since he couldn't guarantee that.

Although the team was unsettled by the departure, this communication answered their questions and they quickly resettled back into the regular cadence of their work.

Through his communication, Ryan shared that Marshall had been treated with respect. He maintained the director's privacy while still providing a reason for the departure. He demonstrated that he valued the employees by communicating the situation directly to them and calmed any concerns they may have had.

When terminations haven't been well communicated like this, I've seen the remaining employees create fear-based explanations for the exits that are damaging to the corporate culture. These explanations have been "It's all part of a bigger plan to close the office," "They're going to outsource our department," or "The new boss is going to replace the whole team with his chosen recruits." The unsupported justifications are often wrong but still cause a lot of unnecessary stress.

Ryan avoided these types of rumors by solidly delivering the message that jobs were safe as long as the employees performed in their role. The honesty in Ryan's message rang true to the team.

Stepping away from the specifics of the story, if the truth is employees have been let go because the business is facing financial challenges and evidence of these difficulties are apparent to the staff, such as customer losses, the leader's message should be honest about this and the potential future implications. However, the communication should include a plan to improve the company's performance and actions the employees can take to support the plan.

Some readers may view admitting that a company is in a difficult situation as a risk since it could reduce the workforce's commitment to the organization. However, I believe if signs of challenges are visible and leaders are silent about it, this will only damage trust and increase uncertainty and stress. That anxiety could push some individuals to commence a job search anyway. If leaders are direct, employees will believe they'll be informed if situations worsen and be treated fairly. As a result, they'll be more engaged and likely to make efforts to improve the situation rather than jump ship as soon as they can.

Providing clarity around terminations, within privacy limitations, is an opportunity to build trust with a workforce and will reduce the distractions and productivity losses that can otherwise ensue after employee exits.

Authentic Company Identity

Clearly communicating what a business aspires to be and how it will achieve its goals will create clarity and certainty of a company's identity. Understanding this identity means current and prospective employees won't have to work to piece the story together through observations and rumors. This leaves greater focus toward fulfilling corporate objectives.

A Clear Mission and Vision

Companies with a well-defined purpose through their mission and vision will have a more motivated and secure workforce than those businesses who lack a clear direction. Clarity around the business's mission will give employees confidence in leadership and the future of the organization. As a result, they can fully focus on their work.

Corporate Values

Corporate values portray what's important to those at the company, what its leaders will consider in their decision-making processes, and how people will be treated by those within the organization. If corporate values align with the words and actions of leaders, it will create comfort and security for employees as they can trust decisions will be made based on those values.

Company Objectives and Individual Goals That Are Clear and Aligned

Establishing individual goals that align with the overall organization's mission and objectives will demonstrate that the employee is needed and will increase their job security. Leaders must also be aware that depending on the situation, certain goals may create insecurity. For example, in times of uncertainty, stretch goals may increase an employee's insecurity and have the opposite intended effect of lowering performance instead of achieving exceptional results.

Performance Management

Employees will have greater security in their roles if they know whether they are meeting performance expectations, and if they aren't, they are clear on the improvements needed and feel they are supported to make these improvements.

General Communication

To achieve sufficient transparency and security for employees, there must be alignment between what leaders say and what they do, critical messages must be sent frequently and through multiple channels, the reasoning behind decisions should be shared, and follow-up opportunities created.

Communication of Layoffs and Terminations

Transparency in the communication of layoffs and terminations will avoid employees becoming insecure about their own job and will reduce the productivity losses as they try to understand why a peer was let go and what it means for the business.

CHAPTER 9

THE IMPACT OF POOR HIRING AND PROMOTION DECISIONS

Creating a psychologically safe work environment and acting to minimize factors that create uncertainty are critical to support productivity and growth. However, even in a healthy, stable workplace, other aspects of an employee's role can magnify insecurities and impact their performance.

We experience our personal situation first; therefore, in the context of the workplace, our comfort in our role is the primary influence on our mental state and the environment is secondary. If our job itself creates significant insecurities, those feelings may not be calmed regardless of the health of the work environment.

This chapter outlines common issues that may cause us to feel insecure in our roles leading to anxiety, stress, and lower performance.

WHEN PERSONALITY OVERRIDES OBJECTIVE INTERVIEWING

A successful hire or promotion achieves a match between the knowledge and skills required for a role and those that the selected candidate brings to it. That match is critical, both for the company to benefit from the successful performance of the role and for the new employee to feel secure in their position.

The need for this skills match sounds both self-evident in its importance and straightforward to achieve. Unfortunately, the priority of the alignment of needs and skills is often sidelined during the interview process. The power of personal impressions and interpersonal dynamics can influence the interview and distract from the reality of the role. Markus's experience in this next story is an example of this.

> Markus met with Tara about an opportunity to join her growing business. Tara was the CEO of Company R, an e-commerce startup. She felt she needed a chief operating officer (COO).
>
> Markus had been COO at one of Company R's competitors, so Tara was eager to have him join the team and share his valuable experience. However, Company R was at a much earlier stage in its life cycle than Markus's last employer. The role would be more hands-on than Markus's previous position.
>
> The interview process was extremely casual. Among other

high-level topics, Tara asked Markus about his leadership style and shared the business's strategy but didn't get into the tactical aspects of the role. Markus liked Tara's energy and excitement about the company and saw himself working well with her. The idea of helping Company R overtake his old employer was also quite attractive to Markus.

Markus asked questions about Company R's long-term vision and funding plans but failed to ask about the day-to-day of the job. Given his experience in the industry, Markus assumed he knew what the role would entail.

After an excellent two-hour discussion, both Markus and Tara were sold. Next, Markus met with the HR director and the CFO. Those discussions were also future-oriented and filled with excitement. Markus got a great vibe from the team and accepted the job offer.

Within a week of joining the company, Markus realized the predicament he was now facing. Given the startup phase, his department didn't have the technology and automation that he was used to. Most of the processes were manual, and as a result, operational data was incomplete and not as timely as he would like.

Markus was used to having data available at his fingertips. He would have to build and staff new systems to make that possible here. Additionally, system selection and implementation weren't Markus's strong suit; he'd had a team to look after that at his last job. This company didn't have that skillset or the funds to hire the necessary talent.

Markus questioned whether he had sold himself incorrectly in the interview process. He was a strategy guy, not an execution guy. This role needed execution. Markus began to lose sleep as he struggled to figure out how to meet the company's needs. For four months, he attempted to make it work. The only result was the deterioration of his mental health.

At the end of the fourth month, Markus sat down with Tara and explained that he simply wasn't what the business needed. Tara had been watching his lack of progress, too, and had been hoping that success would come. She couldn't deny that it wasn't working.

Tara recognized the blame was shared. She'd been so caught up in Markus's impressive résumé and their instant personal connection that she hadn't considered if the company was truly ready for his skills. Now four months had passed, significant dollars had been spent, and she would have to go back on the hunt for the right candidate.

Before starting the recruitment, Tara planned to consider whether a COO was actually what she needed. Given the tactical aspects of the role, she now realized a director of operations candidate may be more aligned with the requirements of the position. This time, she would ensure she targeted the right skillset and level of experience for the needs of the business.

INADEQUATE ANALYSIS AND COMMUNICATION OF POSITION REQUIREMENTS

Tara hadn't put enough thought into exactly what the company needed in the senior operations role. As a result, she was easily distracted by Markus's background and personality, even though his skillset wasn't the right fit.

This scenario isn't uncommon. As experienced professionals, we often assume that we know what roles need because we've been in our field for so long. Or in some cases, we may be hiring for a position that we aren't an expert in. We think we understand the requirements of the role, but in reality, we don't, and can't, without systematically analyzing them.

I've been recruited for finance roles by CEOs who weren't involved in the day-to-day running of the finance department. In those situations, when I asked to speak to someone who was actually on the finance team at the company, those discussions often revealed that the reality of the job differed significantly from the CEO's portrayal of it.

I've found that senior leaders who aren't involved in the minutiae of the roles they are recruiting for can unintentionally gloss over the less desirable aspects of the positions. They truly might not be aware of them. However, if we aren't completely clear on the competencies and traits required for a position, we risk misrepresenting what the job involves. Or we also risk being easily swayed by candidates whose personality we like but that don't have the actual skills the role needs or the desire to perform the tasks required for the position.

The positive connection formed by Markus and Tara blinded them to the mismatch between Markus's experience and seniority level and the needs of Tara's company. Markus didn't have the needed skills, and Tara couldn't offer him the team he needed to fill those gaps in order to be successful.

A skills mismatch may function but not as well as it could have with the right candidate. In a worst-case outcome, the person is completely wrong for the role. That level of mismatch can negatively impact the person hired, the others on the team, customers, and the overall business. The employee is likely to become insecure as they try to meet expectations without the necessary tools.

We saw how this type of situation can magnify insecurity in the example of Tom in Chapter 4. Tom procrastinated about completing his product budget because he didn't feel competent in his forecasting abilities. This resulted in a poor budget submission, an unfavorable review by his boss, and the deepening of Tom's insecurity. The person who hired Tom likely didn't identify during the recruitment process that Tom had a competency gap in financial forecasting. Therefore, Tom was left to manage the forecasting without support, and this had a detrimental effect.

I've observed that this scenario creates a vicious circle. The self-doubt that comes along with insecurity can cause someone hired into the wrong role to blame themselves for not understanding what the role required. As a result, they may hide their difficulties and try to figure out what is needed without support. If this effort is unsuccessful, it will only magnify their insecurities. This can make the situation difficult to correct since the employee may become defensive and avoidant of the problem.

RESPONSIBILITY DRIFT

A skills mismatch isn't just something that happens when someone is first hired at a company. It can also gradually occur over time. Employees' responsibilities may drift into new areas as their roles change. This may happen when someone leaves the organization and their responsibilities are distributed among the remaining staff. Alternatively, as the business evolves and grows, additional tasks may be assigned and/or the complexity of existing tasks may increase.

These changes create opportunities for career growth, but too often, tasks are assigned without assessing the level of training needed to execute them or the impact of the new tasks on an employee's existing workload. If leaders aren't cautious with the assignment of additional tasks, employees may be given responsibilities they don't have the competencies for without the necessary support or the time to do them well.

There are several situations in which responsibility drift can occur:

New leaders may not attempt to learn in detail the skillsets or workloads of the team in place when they join a company: in my experience, new leaders rarely perform a thorough review of the backgrounds or capacity of their new team. They may not want to make their subordinates feel threatened by the fact that their boss is reviewing their skillset and work. Alternatively, a recently arrived leader may be too caught up in learning their role to systematically orient themselves to their team's capabilities, so they take the short-cut of making assumptions. The result is that employees' abilities are often over- or underestimated.

Both under- and overestimation of skill levels can have negative consequences, but if greater than actual experience is assumed, the employee may be too nervous to say that they don't have the competencies needed to take on assigned tasks. Or they are ambitious to grow their careers, and so remain silent about the misunderstanding for fear they will lose the opportunity. Instead, they take on the tasks and hope to figure them out. Taking these on without support could lead to poor performance or outright failure, and new insecurities.

Existing leaders may allocate tasks without thoughtful consideration of skills and workloads: although responsibility drift is more likely under a new leader who didn't hire the employees, it can also occur under an existing leader who allocates additional tasks without adequate forethought.

Leaders are often very busy and simply want to give tasks to the person they think will get them done. However, if they don't look beforehand at the impact on the assignee's overall workload, they may burden an employee with too much to accomplish. Or they may assume a high-performing team player has the skills to take on a particular task when in actuality the employee has a competency gap in that area. Tasks get allocated without determining whether the assignee needs support or training and whether the resources to provide them are available.

The outcome in both scenarios is an employee who's isn't set up for success. High performers may figure out how to get the tasks done, but their experience would be far less stressful if they were provided with the needed support and training.

Business growth may increase the complexity and volume of work: an employee may experience changes in their role as their company grows. The responsibilities of a position may become more complex as the general needs of the business expand. Someone hired to manage a department in an organization with $1 million of revenue may not be able to handle the far greater complexity when revenue grows to $20 million and then $100 million.

I saw this kind of change when I was a controller at a junior mining company. We progressed from our shares trading on a junior stock exchange to trading on both the larger stock exchange in our jurisdiction as well as listing on a foreign stock exchange.

This required shorter timelines for financial reporting and stricter regulatory compliance. The complexity of my responsibilities significantly increased although the role itself stayed the same as financial controller.

Fortunately, I had been advancing my education throughout this period, so I was able to adapt to the increased demands. My boss also observed the changes and allowed me to add a team member to assist with the additional work. If my leader hadn't been continually assessing my workload and the changing requirements as the company grew, I could have easily gotten in over my head.

Job descriptions may not always have changed, but the volume, timelines, and difficulty of tasks may transform and create challenges. This can trigger insecurity as the employee faces managing a job they were once able to do and now are struggling with.

If these situations occur in a toxic work environment, the impacted employee may be unwilling to ask for help for fear of exposing a weakness. This is detrimental to the business as objectives may not be met. The employee is also likely to use defensive behaviors which can further damage the already poor work environment.

OVERPROMOTION

Overpromotion differs from responsibility drift in that it's a conscious decision by a leader to advance an employee rather than a sometimes accidental or unnoticed progression of responsibilities into new areas or more complex work. It's the promotion of an employee to a position they aren't ready for. They may lack either the necessary experience or competencies, or both. A common result is that the employee struggles to perform and suffers psychologically as a result.

Rachel's situation in this next story is a clear example of overpromotion.

Rachel had joined Company Y during its startup phase as its bookkeeper. The business grew significantly. Rachel was very proud when they offered her the role of controller. She didn't mind that her salary was far below market for someone with that title; she was excited for the opportunity. Rachel had never led a team before or implemented the systems that would be required to manage the growth, but she was looking forward to the experience.

Unfortunately, Rachel didn't have a mentor, and she was left on her own to make decisions. The situation deteriorated quickly. Although she was working hard, Rachel lacked knowledge and experience. She set up dysfunctional systems and processes. She hired a team, but none of the new employees had set up the needed processes or systems before either. Rachel recruited people whom she could mentor, not realizing that what she needed was a staff to help her.

Rachel saw that her team wasn't meeting expectations. She worked even harder to improve. However, without the necessary support and capabilities, she wasn't able to make the changes needed for success. Every day, Rachel's insecurity about her performance increased.

Company Y's leadership team saw that Rachel was struggling and decided it was time to invest in a senior finance executive. Graham was hired as CFO. He quickly saw that Rachel had been put into her role for the wrong reason: affordable salary instead of experience.

By now, Rachel was deeply insecure about her performance.

She became defensive when Graham provided feedback and made changes.

Given the short window of time for success in a startup environment, Graham didn't have the luxury of mentoring Rachel. He let her go and hired someone with the senior-level experience that was needed for the controller position from the beginning.

Although Graham communicated the reason for the termination as kindly and practically as possible, the termination was devastating for Rachel and compounded her insecurities. She found another job but to this day hasn't reached the level of success that she was aiming for. The knock to her confidence from her experience at Company Y has likely played a part.

Rachel had perpetuated the mistake made by Company Y's leaders in placing her in the position by hiring other inexperienced people. Graham terminated a second individual due to insufficient skills, damaging their confidence and extending the negative outcomes of the initial poor decision to promote Rachel.

Overpromotion doesn't always have a bad outcome. At times, we take chances on people and they excel. All of us need to be challenged to grow and promotions provide those challenges. However, this success typically occurs when the areas in which the employee will need support are identified and a strategy to provide this help is established. Alternatively, the person may have a strong mentor to provide guidance and give them confidence.

I accepted a promotion to oversee the corporate finance department of an organization although I didn't yet have experience in this area. But it was known that I would have a lot to learn. ~~ support was established to help me gain the knowle~

My employer knew what I brought to the table and what I didn't. As a result, they enabled my success. This worked.

But that experience isn't what always occurs. Often, especially in smaller companies or startups, an employee is thrown into a "sink or swim" situation. If they can swim, the overpromotion can catapult their career. But if they don't have the tools and aren't given the complementary support to do the job, their failures can breed massive insecurity and then snowball. They may become afraid to make decisions, reluctant to ask for help, and weak leaders.

There is shared blame for this. A company that elevates someone as a result of inattentiveness to the skills match or the desire to save on payroll takes part of the responsibility. However, overpromotion is sometimes the result of candidates, including me at certain times in my career, craving advancement for the money, growth, prestige, and validation it offers, so they accept a position they're not suited for with eyes wide shut. (This behavior is the flip side of insecurity and fear of failure inhibiting someone from going for a promotion.) A need to improve our self-worth causes us to ignore or deny that we may not be ready for the added responsibility and thus ill-equipped to fulfill the demands of the role.

This drive for advancement can make individuals consciously choose to follow the frequently championed career growth strategy "Fake it until you make it." In this case, the person seeking promotion isn't tricking themselves into believing they're ready for advancement—they are quite intentionally presenting themselves as prepared for the role when they're actually not. They assume (hope) they'll figure out the job once they're in it.

You won't be surprised to hear that I'm not an advocate of this tactic. Hiding weaknesses or areas of inexperience means the employee won't get proper training, mentorship, or support, and that simply doesn't make sense to me. This approach also requires that we convince others that we're someone that we aren't, which can exacerbate underlying insecurity and feed the development of impostor syndrome. Those feelings may stay with us for our entire career; we'll always have a sense that we faked our way to where we are.

If we hide our weaknesses, we commit ourselves to learning the hard way, creating unnecessary scars and missing out of the tips and tricks of those more experienced than we are. Those factors increase the risk that we will underperform, harming our careers and also damaging our professional relationships if people determine that we misrepresented ourselves.

In the startup phase, rather than using limited financial resources to hire candidates with experience, these companies often take chances on unproven people whom they hope are versatile and fast learners. In doing this, they risk hiring people who are following the fake-it strategy. Or they take advantage of those who are eager for growth so are willing to take on responsibilities that are known to be beyond their experience and skillset.

In one example, a startup was aiming to do as much as possible with as little as possible. As a result, a single individual was hired to manage the entire marketing function in the role of marketing director. This included digital marketing, public relations, general marketing, and branding. The person placed in the role had only a few years of marketing experience, which was primarily in digital marketing. They valiantly tried to stretch in the role, but having such a large mandate and limited experience made it difficult to do anything to the level of performance needed.

As it became increasingly apparent that expectations weren't being met, the marketing director became insecure and defensive. Their reaction made it difficult for their leader to provide feedback to improve performance. The situation ultimately was unsalvageable, and the employee was let go. Trying to have one inexperienced person wear all the marketing hats wasted time and money for the company and both the business and the employee were hurt by the outcome.

In other cases, overpromotion can be a means by which a leader ensures that a position that should be operating with independent authority is reliant on them for decision making, thereby ceding the independence of the role. In one case I learned of, a CEO promoted an HR generalist with no leadership experience to the role of vice-president, HR, overseeing more than two hundred staff. The result was a head of HR, who should have been advocating for the people, needing to consult the CEO on every decision and taking the CEO's advice in all situations.

As a result, the employees saw HR as an extension of the CEO rather than the department looking out for the overall corporate culture. The culture was already toxic before the promotion, and the new VP didn't make any changes to improve it; they simply executed what the CEO wanted.

Other reasons for overpromotion are:

- A poor assessment was made of what the higher-level role requires.
- A biased personal preference for an internal candidate overpowers the hiring manager's ability to acknowledge the candidate's lack of relevant experience.

- A promotion is given to an employee as a reward for a job well done in their current position without assessing their ability to succeed in the new role.
- A job is awarded to a family member, friend, or past colleague without concern for their ability to perform it. The term for this is nepotism.
- A promotion is given based on seniority rather than ability.

Regardless of the route to the overpromotion, as shared, the impacts can be detrimental to the company and the employee. These effects will be even greater if the person is advanced to a leadership position they aren't prepared for.

If they are a leader, their conduct will not only impact their work but also their team. If someone isn't ready to move to an oversight role that requires strategy, problem solving, and the ability to take responsibility for the performance of others, this is likely to trigger their insecurities. When the employee realizes they're in over their head, they may use dysfunctional management styles, such as micromanagement, to assert dominance and control, as well as use the defensive behaviors outlined in Chapters 3 and 4.

In addition, as Company Y experienced when Rachel hired her team, if an underqualified person is building a team without any guidance, they may do so with equivalently underqualified people. This can be the result of inexperience; sometimes it can be because, at a subconscious level, they don't want to hire candidates who have a skill level above theirs. This creates a cascading effect of underqualified employees on a team. The effect is magnified when the leader is not able to support their inexperienced team because they're so focused on their own struggle to perform adequately.

The negative impact of the overpromotion can extend beyond the underperforming leader and team: other employees may lose confidence in a company where underqualified people are consistently advanced. They recognize the business isn't staffed with people they can learn from and lose faith in the organization's ability to perform if it isn't investing in the right people. They will be inclined to leave for better-managed companies that offer greater job security and opportunities for professional growth.

VALUES MISMATCH

Misalignment between an employee's values and the values of their employer can be at least as detrimental to a business or an individual as a skills mismatch. Tracey's story highlights the cost of this incompatibility to a candidate who was misled during the hiring process.

Tracey was considering joining Company O as finance manager but wasn't entirely certain whether the corporate culture was the right fit for her. Company O's CFO wanted Tracey to join the team, so he arranged for her to meet with the organization's HR director, Alana. He gave Alana the task of convincing Tracey to accept the position.

Tracey wanted to work for a company with the philosophy that happy employees and a healthy culture were critical to the success of the business. She shared this desire with Alana. Alana told Tracey that this was in fact Company O's philosophy.

Alana shared that the business had been through a tough time after restructuring but assured Tracey they were turning a corner. Tracey had been through restructuring in a previous position, so she knew the instability and dysfunction it causes. She believed Alana that Company O's plan was to engage the whole team in building a positive and healthy corporate culture compatible with her values. Tracey accepted the position on this basis.

On her first day, very few people came to welcome Tracey. She walked through the office, and no one looked up to greet her. This was definitely a culture that needed work, she thought. Yet, she still believed Alana's assurances.

Month after month, the managers meetings went by with the discussions revolving around profitability and cost cutting. Tracey kept expecting Alana to raise cultural initiatives, but very little about improving the culture was ever mentioned. Instead, Tracey learned that additional layoffs were planned and that cuts were being made to existing benefits.

Tracey tried to do her part to improve the work environment. But because she was an unknown quantity to the other employees, they neither trusted her nor responded to her efforts.

It didn't take long for Tracey to conclude she had been misled; the company's focus was purely on cutting costs to increase profitability, not on supporting its people.

Tracey's trust in the CFO and HR director disappeared. The loss of trust obliterated any remaining sense of security. Despite that, Tracey didn't leave the company right away because she didn't want a short stint on her résumé. She moved on shortly after her one-year anniversary.

Tracey's experience with Company O isn't uncommon. When trying to recruit a desirable candidate, some hiring managers misrepresent their true corporate cultures or paint the culture in a *highly* positive light. In fact, a Glassdoor survey reported that 61 percent of their respondents had found aspects of a new job to be different from the expectation set during the interview process; the corporate culture was cited as what differed the most (DePaul 2020).

If a hiring manager tells a candidate whatever they need to hear to get them in the door, among other mismatches, candidates seeking a people-first culture may inadvertently join a profit-first culture. The hiring manager may think they can smooth over any issues once the candidate has joined the company. However, when the employee realizes they were misled, their trust in leadership will be reduced and will be difficult to rebuild.

This situation happened to me. I specifically chose one employer because the values they promoted aligned with mine, only to discover upon joining that the values were mere window dressing. The company's leaders led with fear, which created a psychologically unsafe and toxic work environment.

I stayed at the company for nearly two years because I felt I had to for the sake of my résumé. Looking back on it now, although a lot of movement on a résumé isn't ideal, neither is stagnating in a position that isn't right for us. I should have left when I realized the culture had been misrepresented to me.

Although short stints on résumés can be difficult to explain, so is lack of progress. Our performance quality will drop because of poor motivation in an environment that we don't fit into. This will limit our career growth and our desire to learn. We will be much more likely to develop our careers in a workplace that aligns with our values and goals.

Hiring managers may think getting their desired candidate is worth all efforts, even misleading someone. But no matter the skills and background of the employee, they won't contribute at their highest level in an organization that doesn't align with their values.

TITLE MISALIGNMENT WITH RESPONSIBILITIES OR COMPANY STRUCTURE

In my opinion, another aspect of placing candidates in the right job is having an accurate title for that position. I often hear people say that titles don't matter. I've said it myself in the past, but over time I've learned that as much as I wish they didn't, they do. And insecurities can be created in relation to them.

Rightly or wrongly, titles are how people classify each other. It's important to be aware of the impact the label we give an employee has on them, their coworkers, and the organizational structure overall.

Angela's experience in the following story is an example of how titles matter in our society.

> Angela was controller for a mining company developing a $500 million mining operation in Peru. Her friend Jennifer was CFO of a small mineral exploration company with a $1 million budget.
>
> They went to a networking event together. Everyone they met at the event was impressed by Jennifer's title and praised her for reaching such a high level, when in reality Angela had greater responsibility and complexity to manage as controller at a much larger development-stage mine.

Of course, most people don't understand the different phases of mining, so they measured the peers on the basis they could appreciate, their titles. From this story, you can see how the recognition we get from perceived high-level titles can drive individuals to ask for them. Our society places a significant emphasis on labels, so the weightier the label sounds, the greater our social status.

Because of their power, it's common for senior titles to be given as rewards or as forms of compensation. This occurs even when the title is more senior than the level of actual work required or the experience needed to do a job. This is particularly the case in startup companies with limited budgets; a prestigious moniker is handed out rather than paying a higher salary.

Most people want these senior titles and the associated stature that goes with them. However, they and their employer don't often realize the issues a misrepresentation of their role may cause further down the road.

Potential employers use a candidate's last title to help them classify the candidate: hiring managers use the former title to understand what candidates have done. If the title doesn't accurately represent the duties of their last job, the person may get a position they aren't ready for. This can result in the same effects as overpromotion.

Employees may not be considered for the roles they're actually qualified for: a candidate with an inflated title may be assumed to be overqualified for a position that's actually the right fit. In speaking to recruiters, I've learned they sometimes recommend to candidates that they reduce the level of an exaggerated title on their résumé to ensure they're considered for the opportunities they're qualified for.

If the business grows, the company may truly need a person with the skills and experience normally associated with that title: if the truth is, the person given the title doesn't have the abilities expected of someone in that position, it can later become glaring if those skills are needed. If that happens, the company has to decide whether to demote the person (damaging their confidence), let the person go (damaging their confidence), or create a position with an equivalently senior designation and awkwardly fit it into their organizational structure.

Employees can become upset if they see the titles of their peers as misaligned: employees expect those with more prominent titles than themselves to have greater responsibility, experience, and/ or competencies than them. If they don't see this, they'll think it's unfair and feel they should also have a senior-level ranking. This can damage trust in leaders and create toxicity in the environment.

Maxwell's story demonstrates the negative impacts that can occur when insufficient thought is put into the structure of titles within an organization.

> Maxwell was recruiting for the role of manager of product for his company. He'd found an ideal candidate, Lana, but Lana held the director of product position at her current employer and wanted to maintain that title. However, Lana agreed on the salary offered. So Maxwell figured that if it didn't cost him anything and secured his desired candidate, it was an easy decision.
>
> Maxwell failed to consider that the business didn't have a director level in their structure. They were a small group, so each department had a manager who reported into either himself as CTO or to the other C-suite executives (CEO, COO, or CFO).
>
> After he announced Lana's hire, the executives had multiple managers ask to discuss their roles and say they felt their role held the same importance as the director of product role. They wanted to understand why they didn't have the director label as well.

> Privately, the managers talked among themselves about why Lana, who hadn't proven herself yet, had earned this title. They speculated whether Lana had a higher salary than them.
>
> Maxwell missing the importance of titles forced the executives to revisit all their managers' roles and compensation. This review highlighted that some employees deserved a director position and a salary increase, which they were given.
>
> However, a role change wasn't justified for some managers. Those employees were left feeling like they were treated unfairly. The truth was that Lana's role and experience didn't truly merit a director title. Maxwell had simply carried forward the inaccurate moniker Lana had been given in her last role.
>
> When Lana started, she had no idea of the furor her title had caused. She felt tension in the environment and people weren't as friendly with her as she expected, but she didn't know why.

As Maxwell experienced, allocating titles for the wrong reasons can cause problems within the company's workforce. As leaders, we can't overlook that every decision we make can have unintended consequences. We may think we're just giving someone a better title. What could it hurt? That is, until we truly need the skillset typically required of someone in that position and must decide what to do, or we're faced with a number of newly insecure people wondering why their role isn't worthy of a similar ranking.

This can result in issues of comparison and jealousy, as outlined in Chapter 4, creating a situation in which working relationships are negatively impacted by the insecurity that the perceived unfairness in titles creates. This is likely what Lana was feeling in the tension of the work environment.

UNFAIR TREATMENT OF EMPLOYEES

All of us deserve to be treated fairly, but fair treatment can mean something different to each of us. In the context of employment, fairness is a factor in three main areas: career growth, compensation, and workload.

Unfairness in Opportunities for Career Growth

I've found that those who aspire to climb a corporate ladder tend to be open to sacrifice. They will take on extra work for less pay while they build their careers and invest in relationships that will catapult them closer to the top.

I've heard few concerns about hours and compensation from ambitious people pushing their way up the corporate ladder, as they seem to realize achieving their goals will require this sacrifice in the short term. They accept this in their drive for promotions and learning opportunities.

I did this very thing early in my career. I felt the need to prove myself, so I took on any task presented to me and didn't worry about my pay or hours. I don't necessarily advocate for this approach since we all deserve to be paid fairly for our time. However, the reality is that early in our careers, this sacrifice can give us the experience needed to grow and learn.

Of course, promotion opportunities must eventually come to fruition, but many of us will willingly work long hours if the promise seems real. However, many companies don't have structured plans for employee progression, so those giving their time assume the cause and effect of hours spent to career growth. If advancement doesn't come as we expect for ourselves but it does for others, we may see the success of those coworkers as unfair. This can cause toxicity and insecurity in the workplace.

An employee who was once committed to their job and striving for growth can feel slighted, lose trust in leadership, and become jealous of their peers. Research has shown that the perception of an event as unfair can cause hostility and undermines trust (Rock 2016). For this reason, a company that leaves career progression open to interpretation and perception, rather than creating clarity around it, risks a toxic work environment.

Unfairness in Compensation

Although reaching our full potential at work and climbing the corporate ladder is attractive, for some, other aspects of life take priority, such as exploring the world, family, or nonwork hobbies. There is nothing wrong with this. Employers can have long successful working relationships with people whose primary focus isn't promotions and career growth. However, these employees still have priorities that require fairness. Their priorities are wages and time commitments or workload. An imbalance in these two elements is what can create insecurity for them.

Even those who are focused on growing their careers will eventually become disenchanted with an employer who doesn't pay them fairly for their time. Even the benefit of promotions and bigger titles will begin to pale if someone is being paid below market and unreasonable demands are being put on their time.

Rosalie's story demonstrates the impact when an employee feels they aren't being paid fairly.

Rosalie joined Company C as operations coordinator after earning a two-year operations management degree. She had many years of administrative experience, but the degree was her first postsecondary credential. Rosalie knew she'd exceed the expectations of a typical graduate from a two-year program, who would have little prior experience to offer.

Rosalie had accepted the position and its low-end market salary with the hope that she'd prove her worth and be given a salary increase. Rosalie performed extremely well in her role, exactly as she expected; within two months of joining Company C, her responsibilities had grown well beyond the original job description.

Rosalie's duties continued to expand as her boss realized what she was capable of. However, months passed and her salary wasn't discussed.

At the six-month mark, Rosalie asked for a meeting with her boss to discuss her position. In the meeting, she demonstrated the evolution of her role and the expansion of her job description. He responded by telling her that the company didn't consider salary increases until an employee had been on the payroll for twelve months.

Rosalie was disheartened. Even a small increase would have been a nice gesture to show that she was valued. However, she accepted the policy decision and waited until the twelve-month mark.

At twelve months, she hoped she would be presented with a salary increase as acknowledgment of her contribution. Yet, the twelve-month point came, and additional weeks went by with nothing said.

At fourteen months, Rosalie asked for another meeting with her boss and again laid out her contribution, which had grown further since their last discussion. This time, the leader's response was, "We're completing the annual compensation review in two months, so we'll look at your compensation at that time."

Rosalie was beyond disheartened this time. She felt that her work wasn't being valued. Her trust in her boss diminished since he'd told her that he would review her salary after twelve months. Her motivation decreased. Why would she want to take on more responsibility when she wasn't getting paid to do so?

She found herself looking closely at jobs posted on LinkedIn and wondering if she should go elsewhere. Yet, she held off. She liked her peers in her current role, and it was only two more months until the salary assessment.

The salary reviews finally came, and Rosalie was presented with a letter with the result of the review. She opened the document hopefully, but her heart sank as she saw the number: a 5 percent increase.

Rosalie went to her boss to discuss what she felt was an inadequate raise. He responded, "You should be happy with that increase. It's a real sign that we value you—most people only got 3 percent."

Rosalie didn't care what "most people" got. Her contribution to Company C had doubled in the time she'd been there, and she had been hired at low market or even below market for her skills. She felt that she was being treated unfairly and her commitment to her employer disintegrated.

Instead of just looking at those jobs on LinkedIn, she now hit "Apply" and submitted her résumé. She quickly had multiple

> interviews set up and soon received three job offers between 20 to
> 30 percent higher salary than her current pay. She accepted one
> of them and left Company C.

It's not the employer's responsibility to unburden its employees of financial pressure, as we all make our own lifestyle choices, but it is their responsibility to pay fairly (based on market salaries) for the work done. Company C ignored that the additional responsibilities Rosalie had taken on increased her value in the market, forcing Rosalie to risk going elsewhere or accept what was offered. This deteriorated her trust in management.

The message Company C delivered was that they didn't value Rosalie. It's as if Rosalie's leader was saying, "I can get someone else quite easily, so I am not afraid of losing you." If someone said that to you, it would be difficult not to question your value and doubt yourself.

According to research, the perception of being underpaid doubles the probability that a worker will report experiencing "stress, depression and problems with emotions," and it amplifies other stresses and affects sleep quality (Schieman 2015). In my experience, the performance of an underpaid employee is also likely to deteriorate. They may become insecure and exhibit some of the behaviors outlined in Chapters 3 and 4, such as reduced focus on their work and passive aggressiveness.

I have certainly felt myself distracted and less motivated in my roles when I knew I was earning below market for my skills and contribution. I'm generally not motivated by money, but I *am* motivated by fairness. If I learn that I'm not being compensated fairly, I will feel unsettled until the balance is restored.

To bring the balance back to a perceived fair level, some employees may reduce the effort they put into their work. Someone who believes they are underpaid may stick to a nine-to-five schedule and not have a willingness to go the extra mile. They may also look for jobs elsewhere, as their commitment to a company they perceive as treating them unfairly will not be high.

Unfairness in Workload

Creating a fair compensation structure is crucial, but employees also need to see that allocation of work is equal and workloads are reasonable. By "equal," I mean that certain positions aren't loaded with work while others can barely fill a day.

In many environments, reliable performers will suffer with a heavy workload since they're trusted to do their work well. Meanwhile, low performers complete the minimum to still be considered productive. Without performance management to avoid this, our best employees may be overly stressed. Toxicity can also be created among teammates due to the lack of fairness in the allocation of work.

We see the impacts of a heavy workload in this next story.

Ellen was an excellent employee who was trusted to get work done. However, this trust had resulted in a heavy burden of work on her plate. She was extremely stressed and frustrated as she looked at her peers who didn't have the same level of work.

She started pushing through tasks to reduce the pressure. One of these tasks was recruiting an Accounts Payable manager that was needed ASAP.

Ellen's schedule was packed with meetings, but she found a

fifteen-minute slot to meet a candidate with the right credentials. The candidate was friendly and presentable, so Ellen hired her without performing any due diligence and she ignored a few red flags. Ellen's need to reduce her burden and get things done overwhelmed the value of the process to ensure the right fit.

This employee became a huge problem calling in sick often, making unreasonable demands, and actually adding to Ellen's heavy workload. In the end, Ellen had to let her go and start the recruitment process all over again, taking up more of her limited time.

Ellen became bitter about the heavy workload that she felt contributed to her mistake. The mistake also hurt Ellen's confidence about her hiring skills and judgment. In truth, her hiring skills were fine; she had just been too busy to use them.

Heavy workloads, like Ellen's, are not uncommon as companies push their staff to stay competitive in dynamic fast-moving markets. Everyone is afraid of being left behind if they aren't as efficient or as innovative as their competitors. This places stress on employees, expecting them to work faster and smarter. However, there is a point of diminishing returns.

Every person reading this has likely experienced a situation similar to Ellen's. You feel so much pressure that you accept the first thing that comes along that looks like it will ease some of that burden. Unfortunately, as in Ellen's case, this often backfires as we don't properly consider the decision. In the end, the bad call can take up more of our time than if we'd slowed down and thought through our choice properly. It can also create insecurity as we blame ourselves for poor judgment.

If we put too much pressure on employees such as crazy tight deadlines and unreasonable expectations, it can cause behaviors that will work against achieving success and the quality of work will drop. Trust in leaders will also diminish and negative emotions around fairness can be created.

WHY THIS MATTERS TO YOU

Skills Mismatch

Even in a healthy environment, if an employee is a bad fit for their position and doesn't have support, it will be challenging for them to feel secure. They won't perform to their full potential and may exhibit toxic defensive behavior as they sense they aren't meeting expectations.

Responsibility Drift

The responsibilities of a position may drift into new areas as leaders change and the company evolves. However, if this occurs without sufficient consideration of skillset and workload, an employee can become overwhelmed by additional tasks. This can create insecurity and lead to poor performance.

Overpromotion

Overpromotion is common in companies who are bias toward lower salaries rather than experience. An overpromoted employee may exhibit dysfunctional behaviors in an effort to compensate for their inexperience. This can significantly impact the health of a work environment, particularly if the person is advanced to a leadership role.

Values Mismatch

If a chosen candidate accepts a position and upon joining realizes the values of those within the organization aren't as they expected, it can create distrust and insecurity. It will also be difficult to motivate and inspire employees whose values don't align with their employer's.

Title Misalignment

Giving out higher level titles than a role merits can cause problems as a company grows. They may actually need a person with the skills and experience normally ascribed to that title. Employees may also have challenges if they later look for positions elsewhere. They may not be considered for roles they are truly qualified for due to their inflated title.

Unfair Treatment of Employees

Fair treatment can mean something different to each of us. However, there are three key areas where fairness is critical: career growth, compensation, and workload. The perception of unfairness in these areas can create insecurity and increase toxicity in the work environment.

CHAPTER 10

STRATEGIES TO HIRE AND MAINTAIN A SECURE WORKFORCE

Now for the good news: all the factors shared in the last chapter that can create insecurity around a role can be prevented. And what's more, most of the actions to avoid these situations aren't costly.

In fact, these actions will save the business money; having the right people in the right roles with appropriate support and an accurate understanding of the organization will reduce the costs of employee turnover. These efforts require thoughtfulness, openness, and awareness but will ensure that employees are confident in their positions and will be productive members of the workforce.

IDENTIFY AND OUTLINE THE NEEDS
OF THE POSITION

Finding the right candidate for a position is one of my favorite parts of being a leader. I enjoy meeting people and hearing their stories, but I also love figuring out who will work well with my team and contribute to a high-performing, positive culture. Adding a person to a team is a big responsibility and I see recruitment as one of a leader's most important tasks. The decision impacts both the new hire's life and the functioning of the existing team. It's not a responsibility to be taken lightly.

Hiring or promoting the ideal candidate starts with clearly defining what is needed in the role. I find the most effective approach is to outline objective evaluation criteria against which to measure all applicants. A defined set of evaluation criteria will reduce the risk of selecting a candidate because of their personality alone or as the result of personal biases. To avoid bias and ensure objectivity, the selection criteria should be developed without a specific candidate in mind.

The hiring criteria should include the technical and interpersonal competencies needed for the position. It's useful to define them as "must-haves" and "nice-to-haves." Consideration of the cultural fit is also critical to ensure a candidate will feel at home at the company. When recruiting for an unfamiliar position, I recommend seeking the advice of someone who has recently held the role or one similar to it. They can explain the true day-to-day details of the job to ensure all the key elements of the position are captured.

Along with defining the evaluation criteria, it's critical to assess the expected workload of the role, particularly if it's a new position.

It's not always easy to judge how long tasks will take or account for all potential outcomes, but the effort should be made to ensure the role is well balanced with short-term and long-term achievable objectives. Having this defined reduces the risk of an excessive workload and sets the candidate up for success.

I consider the following questions to understand the level of experience and mindset needed in the new hire:

- Is a leader available to spend time mentoring the hire?
- Will the person currently in the role, or someone in an equivalent position, be available to pass on information and help train the new person?
- How senior is the team the employee will be working with?
- Is the company expected to grow rapidly so that the person in the role will also be expected to grow and perform quickly?

If answering these questions identifies limited opportunities for training, support, or mentoring opportunities, the hire must be someone who has experience with the specific tasks required or who is proven to be a quick learner and ready for growth. In this situation, if a candidate is recruited who is too junior or is looking for stability rather than a challenge, they may become stressed or insecure when expected to figure out their responsibilities without guidance or are expected to stretch their capabilities in the role.

To determine the character traits best suited to the position and the values that will align with the corporate culture, I consider the following questions:

- What is the style of the team the candidate will be joining? Formal or informal?
- Will the position have autonomy, or will the ability to make decisions be restricted by external factors?
- Does the role require a lot of interpersonal interaction?
- Is the company undergoing change now or will it in the near future? Is its mission stable?
- Will corporate goals and objectives be clear and defined?
- What are the corporate values? What are the behaviors expected of those in the organization?
- What is the level of certainty around daily activities in this position? Will the employee be able to predict how their day will go?

By asking these questions, I consider whether a candidate's personal needs can be met by my company. For example, if the business is in an uncertain startup phase, it's important candidates are aware of the uncertainty and are comfortable with it.

Finally, a common error that can lead to a bad hiring decision is creating too much urgency around the need to fill the role. Typically, the team requiring the recruit says they need the position filled immediately, but it's fairly rare that a company can't wait to find the right fit. Creating a misguided sense of urgency around the recruitment process may cause someone to settle on an applicant who isn't ideal just to get the job filled. This increases the risk of poor candidate selection.

We saw the impact a rushed hire had on Ellen in the last chapter. It increased her stress level and took more time than if she'd waited to find the right person. In the long run, the business would have been better off if it had lowered the pressure on recruitment and waited until they truly found the ideal candidate for the role.

IDENTIFY
COMPETENCY GAPS

Despite accurately defining the selection criteria for a position, it's rare to find the perfect candidate who ticks every box. In light of this, the recruitment process must identify any competency gaps between the role requirements and the applicant's skillset. Isolating these gaps allows the company to confirm whether they have training and/or mentoring resources to support the candidate if they are hired.

For example, if a business is hiring for a leadership position and the organization has excellent leaders who are open to mentoring, then they are able to hire a candidate with less leadership experience than is ideal because they know the existing team can support them and help them grow. If the opposite is true and the company doesn't have a deep leadership bench, hiring a seasoned leader is the right choice—one that incidentally will also strengthen the leadership team.

The identified competency gaps should be explicitly discussed with the candidate before an offer is made. It may seem "off" to discuss an area of perceived weakness with a potential recruit, but again, transparency is important to avoid a hiring mistake. The assessment of competencies and strategies to support the gaps should be clear to both parties. The candidate is likely aware of the elements in their profile that aren't an ideal fit. The knowledge that their future leader is aware of them as well, wants to hire them anyway, and will provide support to help them succeed will actually build the prospective employee's confidence in their ability to take on the new position. They will be more likely to accept if they see that their full profile has been considered and is a good fit despite the areas of weakness.

OFFER FAIR COMPENSATION

We all define fairness differently. However, financial compensation is an area that has objective benchmarks and data that can ensure fair treatment.

Compensation is one of the first agreements that an employer and employee make. For a leader-employee relationship to start off with trust, this agreement needs to be fair to both parties.

Years ago, I was recruiting a junior accountant. When a candidate told me her salary expectations, I recognized it was below the market salary for her experience and skills. The candidate was new to the city and hadn't had time to investigate salaries yet. I could have taken advantage of this and hired her for the salary she proposed, but I recognized she would soon discover it wasn't fair. I told her the request was too low. I hired her and paid her the market wage. She was an excellent, committed employee who was promoted to a higher-level position within a year. If she'd felt I had taken advantage of her from day one, her loyalty and efforts for the business likely wouldn't have been as high.

To ensure the working relationship doesn't start off on the wrong foot, it's essential to investigate the compensation for the specific combination of knowledge, skills, and experience the position requires. If there's uncertainty about the current market salary for a role, I recommend speaking to recruiters or peers or looking at salary surveys.

Once the data has been gathered, it can be used to determine the appropriate compensation package within the organization's budget and compensation policies.

Depending on a company's financial means, fairness may not be achieved through salary alone. If the budget doesn't allow for the level of salary needed to secure the ideal candidate, other options such as vacation time, performance-based bonuses, equity, or growth and training opportunities can be combined to achieve a reasonable compensation package. The critical element is to thoughtfully consider the value the candidate will bring to the business and determine how the organization can provide the candidate with the equivalent value in return.

This thoughtfulness should continue throughout an employee's career with an organization. As they take on more responsibility or as market salaries change, in fairness, when budgets allow, leaders need to be responsive and make corresponding adjustments to their salary package. This will maintain trust and safety in the leader-employee relationship. It will also reduce compensation-related turnover.

THE TITLE MUST FIT
THE ROLE

Titles are challenging since there's no cosmic rule book to tell us the precise level of experience or responsibilities someone should have to merit a particular title or the exact size of the business necessary to justify certain leadership levels.

Every company is different, and every situation has unique aspects. However, as outlined in the "Title Misalignment" section of Chapter 9, the wrong title can have unintended negative consequences on the business, the employee, and the overall team. And as Tara found in her recruitment of Markus, having an incorrect title for a role can also attract the wrong candidates for the position.

Here are some questions to ponder when considering the title for a new job or a change for an existing employee:

- What are the responsibilities and assigned authority of the role? Are these comparable to other positions within the business, and if they are, what are the titles of those jobs? If this is a new title level within the organization, investigate and speak to people in other companies who have this position and consider whether their experience level is the desired fit for the role.

- Is the proposed salary for the position in line with the market for someone with that title?

  - Generally, if the wage for the role is much less than the average market salary for the position, it's a go5-od indicator the person in the role isn't or won't be performing at that level, and the title is therefore not warranted or the salary also needs to be evaluated.

- Does the role have the same impact as others across the organization that are at the same title level?

  - It's important to ensure that individuals at the same title level can perform and contribute along with their peers. Employees at the same perceived level are likely to participate in meetings and training sessions together. They should be able to add value in these situations. Someone who has been given a title far above their experience may become insecure when they can't keep up with their peers.

- If the job title for an employee's current position is being changed, why is the change being considered?
  - Have the responsibilities and/or authority of the current position increased such that the current title no longer aligns with them?
  - Was the title wrong from the outset, and this change is intended to correct the error?
  - Has a change in the role occurred, or is this just a bigger title because the employee wants it? (It's generally a red flag if a change in the role hasn't transpired but a higher title is being considered.)
- For a new hire, is the candidate requesting a more senior title than the position typically commands in the company to align with a title at their last job?
  - If the title level being considered is outside the norm for the company's established organizational structure, contemplate whether this deviation is appropriate. Also, think through the potentially negative reaction from the new hire's functional peers and the cultural impact of that reaction.

Thoughtful consideration of the title and structure of roles within your company can save you from challenges in the long run.

BE HONEST ABOUT THE GOOD AND THE BAD WITH PROSPECTIVE HIRES

If we are thoughtful about the requirements of our open positions and develop clear criteria for the hire, we'll know what we need from a candidate. This is half of the battle. To ensure the correct fit, we also need to meet the candidate's needs and wants. The only way a candidate can decide if a position is right for them is if hiring managers are transparent and present an honest and open reflection of the role, the company, and its culture.

This next story shows how Cathy's transparency resulted in the recruitment of a candidate who understood the challenges they would face in their role. As a result, they were better able to manage them. The employee didn't have distrust layered onto the complexities of the environment.

> Cathy was leading the recruitment for the role of senior finance manager. She interviewed a great candidate, Troy.
>
> Cathy and Troy would be partners, so it was essential to start the relationship with honesty and openness about the organization. The business was going through a difficult time post-acquisition and dealing with the resulting fallout in the workplace culture. Cathy told Troy about the challenges which included high turnover and difficult relationships with their counterparts at the parent company.
>
> Troy still chose to accept the position but did so with his eyes wide open. Cathy and Troy had an excellent working relationship because of this.
>
> Troy did face challenges in his role but never felt resentful because he had been fully informed. He was prepared for the issues. He didn't feel blindsided and could openly discuss any problems with Cathy. That support and transparency made facing any difficulties manageable.

If Troy had joined the company and it wasn't how Cathy had explained, distrust would have been created that would be hard to overcome. To avoid this situation, follow Cathy's lead when hiring: share the good, the bad, and the ugly.

All companies have downsides. Everyone expects an organization to have some issues. However, the issues have to be of a nature that the candidate is prepared to deal with, or they may become resentful and distrustful if they join and discover the situation isn't as they expected.

For example, some people are happy to work overtime hours if it means they have a flexible schedule, while others expect a firm nine-to-five timeline. If an employee expects the conditions to be one way and gets another, they will quickly get disenchanted with their role.

To help a prospective candidate make the right decision, provide an honest overview of the culture, including areas that need to be improved, expected time commitments, and the leadership style of the person they will be working for. If they will be managing a team, provide the makeup of that team and outline any issues that exist there.

I've taken on teams that required a lot of development. However, I was made aware of this during the interview process. I accepted the challenge and focused on improving the team; had I not been given a realistic sense of the situation I was taking on, I would have spent at least some of my valuable time feeling annoyed that I hadn't been fully informed.

We also must be truthful about the company's identity. For example, if a business isn't innovative, that shouldn't be hidden. Employees will quickly figure out that innovation isn't a priority. If an organization is primarily driven by earning profits from existing products rather than creating new ones, the candidate should be told that. There are people who will be driven by either, but these goals will appeal to different personality types.

If the candidate is going to be motivated by what a company has to offer, leaders need to ensure alignment between what drives the business and what drives the candidate. When the true situation isn't well communicated and a mismatch occurs, it will be difficult to motivate the employee.

This total transparency will increase the chance of a great fit and that the company will gain an employee who will be secure and successful in their role and help the business to meet their objectives for years to come.

INTRODUCE NEW HIRES
WITH A STRONG
ONBOARDING PROCESS

Once a candidate is selected and hired, attention should turn to setting them up for success. Unfortunately, I've rarely seen onboarding done well. It often isn't given the importance it deserves. The focus is on ensuring the employee has IT equipment and knows where the bathroom is, rather than ensuring they know the key people in the company and understand the culture, values, products, and priorities of the business. The conventional approach is orientation only; effective onboarding involves all the additional elements.

It's natural for new hires to feel some anxiety and nervousness when they start a job. The onboarding process is an opportunity to establish the work environment as a place of safety where nervousness is calmed and anxiety diminished. If the opposite occurs and an employee ends their first week uncertain whether they made the right decision in joining the company, it will create an insecurity that can be hard to overcome.

Company Q in the next story understood the importance of onboarding. They set Jennica up for success.

Jennica was joining Company Q as customer experience manager. She'd heard great things about the organization, so was excited to see how her first day would go. It exceeded her expectations.

She was told to ask for Mark when she got to the office. He greeted her warmly and said he was her onboarding buddy. He would be her go-to for any general questions or if she just needed a friendly face.

Mark took her through the office and showed her where all the survival basics were located: coffee, water, bathroom, printers, and so forth. After the tour, he showed Jennica to her desk and let the HR specialist, Duncan, know that the first part of her onboarding was complete.

Now it was Duncan's turn. Duncan sat with Jennica for two hours and went over the company's mission, vision, values, policies, and products. He also gave her an overview of the culture and the team she would be joining. He walked her through the organizational chart and identified those she'd be working with. He also gave her insider tips on how to communicate effectively with key people, such as their preferred method of interaction.

Finally, he walked her through the rest of her onboarding plan. She would meet with her new boss, Cassie, next. Then a welcome lunch would be held with her team. That would be it for the day to give Jennica time to process and get settled. The next day, she would have one-to-one sessions with her peers on the team.

> The day after that would be one-to-one sessions with her peers in other departments. From there, Jennica would work directly with Cassie to learn the day-to-day needs of her job and to set objectives. She would have progress check-ins with HR at thirty, sixty, and ninety days.
>
> Jennica felt very good about how thoughtful and thorough the plan was and how much effort the team was putting into setting her up for success. She finished that day and each day that followed increasingly excited by the business and optimistic about her future there.

If an employee is welcomed into a company with the thoughtfulness and structure of Jennica's onboarding plan, they'll feel comfortable in the workplace from the start. They will begin their job with confidence and an understanding of the environment. There's no better time to create that understanding than when an employee first joins the organization.

An effective onboarding program should include:

- An overview of the company's mission, vision, and values.
- An overview of the business's current priorities, such as monthly or quarterly objectives.
- A review of the organizational chart, highlighting the people the employee will work with the most, along with any tips and tricks for working with those people.
- One-to-one sessions with the staff the employee will work closely with.
- An overview of the company's products.
- An assigned buddy, who sits near the new employee, to

be their go-to for questions about the company, day-to-day concerns, and administrative items.

Such efforts significantly help to integrate the new hire into the team environment. They also have the added benefit of reducing the risk of exclusionary behavior. The assignment of a buddy ensures that the employee has someone they "belong" with right from the start and who feels a responsibility to ensure they feel included.

In addition, setting up one-to-ones with multiple people gives the new hire the opportunity to build connections right from day one. These connections will create a sense of belonging and increase the likelihood they'll be included in social activities, such as lunches and after-work events. Also, keep in mind, the new employee isn't the only one who may be nervous about meeting new people; existing employees may feel apprehension as well. Intentionally creating the connections will help everyone.

An employee's first week at work is a critical time to establish their feeling of comfort and safety, not only in their role but also with the business and their peers. It's not a time that a company should take for granted. It can significantly impact someone's future success in the organization.

FACE IT WHEN
YOU DON'T HIRE WELL

As much as we try to recruit the right person into a role, no one will be 100 percent successful in their hiring decisions. When recruitment mistakes are made, it's critical for all involved that we face the facts and correct the situation.

Lynn's story shows what can occur when someone is in the wrong role for their skillset. An employee who isn't meeting expectations can become increasingly insecure and defensive, resulting in further deterioration of their performance.

Lynn hired an administrator, Cassandra, to streamline processes and take over the basic administrative tasks that had been consuming the time of the senior members of Lynn's team.

Cassandra's bright personality was a great fit for the company. However, before long, it became apparent that she struggled with attention to detail. The position required far more detail work than Cassandra's previous job. Her past role was focused on simple office management and keeping employees and visitors in high spirits. She wasn't used to tasks like formatting customer documents and preparing expense reports. She was given feedback, but although she made an effort to improve her work, she continued to produce an unacceptable number of errors.

When Cassandra was given more feedback, she became extremely defensive and insisted that she had improved. Her bright personality dimmed as the knowledge that she wasn't meeting expectations weighed heavily on her.

Lynn waited for four months to see if Cassandra would grow into the role, but the situation only got worse. People had stopped giving Cassandra work; they'd decided it was less hassle to do it themselves. Lynn made the difficult decision that even though she really liked Cassandra, she wasn't the right fit.

When Lynn finally told Cassandra that the role wasn't working out and she was letting her go, she saw the weight lift off her shoulders. The burden of not living up to expectations had been heavy. Cassandra had been anticipating this conversation every day for some time. Lynn had delayed making the call because she felt bad, but every day that she waited had in fact made it harder on Cassandra and the team.

Lynn restarted her recruitment efforts but this time paid careful attention to the candidates' experience with detail-oriented work. She found a candidate who was exactly what the team needed and offered them the position.

Lynn provided Cassandra with a reference and supported her search for a new job. Cassandra found a role where the primary goal was to create a professional, positive office environment. Cassandra was far happier. Everyone was better off once Lynn acknowledged the reality of the situation and made the right decision.

Facing that a change is needed when an employee isn't working out is best for all parties. I've had to restructure teams a number of times over the course of my career, and although I would never say that it's easy, it's definitely become easier. I've realized that when a situation isn't working, it negatively impacts the psychological health of the person who's underperforming and the team around them.

As a matter of workplace fairness, before making any decisions about the role, investigate whether anything in the company's work environment is contributing to the poor performance. Or if the employee's conduct is the issue, a process like that outlined in Chapter 6 under "Dealing with Harmful Behaviors" may be appropriate. If contributing environmental factors aren't identified and the poor performance or conduct is ongoing, it's often best to respectfully exit the individual from the organization.

Most underperforming employees will sense, as Cassandra did, that they aren't meeting expectations. This can create much anxiety and insecurity. After worrying beforehand about how a termination would go, I've even had an employee hug me. They were so thankful to finally be out of an environment that was unmanageable to them.

It often happens that everyone in the workplace (including the problematic employee) knows a situation isn't working and are waiting and wondering when action will finally be taken. I've seen many leaders underestimate the impact an underperforming staff member is having on their coworkers and how obvious it is that a change is needed.

This impact is even greater if the employee is exhibiting toxic behavior. A leader's attempts to be thoughtful and reluctant to hurt that one person may actually be causing significant damage to everyone else on the team. Other team members may be working longer hours to make up for that person's poor work, or the toxicity in the work environment may be negatively affecting their mental health.

It's therefore crucial to consider the welfare of the entire team when deciding the right move in relation to a problematic employee. Otherwise, the organization may lose high performers because of the delay in resolving issues with a low-performing or toxic individual.

Although the termination may be necessary, we still must take responsibility for our poor hiring decision and provide the exited employee with support to find their next role. This may include reasonable severance based on statutory requirements in the relevant jurisdiction and, if needed, assistance with a career search such as résumé or interview support. When these steps are taken, I believe it can result in a fair outcome for all.

It's also important that we learn from poor hiring decisions and take systematic steps to understand the factors that led to the poor fit. This should include an exit interview with the employee to get an understanding of their experience and a review of the hiring process used to select the candidate and of the onboarding process they went through. This review may reveal that steps were missed in the hiring process, such as reference checks, or that onboarding and training was insufficient. These are lessons that can improve the success of future hires.

PROMOTE FROM WITHIN WITH CARE

The original hire of an employee is our first commitment to them, but this responsibility continues throughout their career with our organization. Many employees will desire professional growth and will look for opportunities for advancement. I'm an advocate of promoting from within and have promoted many employees during my career. However, I also believe that we must be cautious in this approach to avoid overpromotion.

Promotion criteria need to be clear and not connected to "time served" but to tangible factors that clearly demonstrate why one person should be selected over another.

As outlined earlier in this chapter, establishing the criteria for a specific position, identifying competency gaps in the candidate's profile, and determining whether the company can offer the necessary support will highlight whether a candidate is the right fit for a role. These same principles should be applied in the consideration of promotions. An internal candidate may be a great cultural fit, but if they don't have the necessary skills or sufficient experience and support resources are lacking, overpromotion is a risk and the individual may be set up for failure or the creation of insecurities.

Darlene's story demonstrates what can occur when thoughtful consideration is put into hiring and internal promotions.

Darlene, who was the vice-president, IT, at her company, had an opportunity available for a network manager. The position would report to the director of networking, who was very experienced and had the bandwidth to mentor.

Darlene's help desk manager, Sam, had been taking courses to grow his career. He was ready for a challenge and was the perfect candidate for the role. Sam understood the business and had the necessary education. It was the ideal promotion scenario, given that the director also had time to mentor him. The role change moved forward.

Now Darlene needed to fill Sam's current role of help desk manager. This was a challenging position, requiring liaising across the organization during a difficult time. The business was in the midst of an operational system upgrade. The role would report to Darlene and she was leading many aspects of the upgrade, so she had limited time to provide mentorship.

An internal candidate, Lucas, applied. A competency gap assessment indicated that he would need training and mentorship that Darlene couldn't offer. Darlene recognized that under the current circumstances, Lucas wasn't the right fit. Darlene selected an external candidate, Louise. Louise was an experienced help desk manager and could hit the ground running.

Darlene explained the reasoning for her choice to Lucas. She also told him that she valued him and wanted to support his continued growth with the company.

Louise performed exactly as Darlene had hoped. She handled all the necessary tasks without training or supervision and also mentored the help desk team, including Lucas. Louise's accomplishments led to the success of the team and supported Darlene's efforts as well.

When Louise moved on from the role two years later, Lucas moved into it. As a result of Louise's mentoring and the additional years of experience, he was now ready for the position.

If Darlene had promoted Lucas too early, it would have been detrimental to the success of the team, the business, Lucas, and herself. By waiting and investing in Lucas, Darlene ensured that everyone succeeded.

The story also demonstrates that if internal employees apply to open positions but aren't selected, it doesn't have to harm their relationship with the company and its leaders. Lucas didn't receive a desired promotion on his initial try, but because Darlene transparently communicated the factors that influenced her choice of Louise, he stayed with the organization and was promoted when he was ready for growth.

This is the process that I recommend when informing someone they didn't get a promotion:

* Once the decision is made, directly inform the employee right away. This way, they don't find out from someone else before they are officially informed.
* Be honest about the reasons they didn't get the position but also share their traits that make them valuable to the company.

- Describe the steps they can take to position themselves for a promotion at a later time.
- If the individual has a future with the company, develop a plan to support their growth. This will demonstrate they are valued.
- Since rejection can be hard to process, check in with the person the next day to reiterate their importance to the business.

Openly communicating the decision-making process and supporting the employee's future will reduce the feelings of self-doubt or unfairness that can otherwise result from missing out on a promotion. They will know the reasons they didn't get the position, rather than being left to imagine the worst and will be motivated to continue performing well and to pursue further professional development.

ROLE EVOLUTION

Having the right people in the right roles is an ongoing challenge as a business evolves through its life cycle. People who were once the right fit for a role may no longer be if the needs of the position change and require a different or higher level of knowledge or skills. Or employees themselves may feel their values or competencies no longer align with the company.

There are many ways an organization can evolve:

- A business that was in the startup stage may experience success and growth that changes its needs. Growth usually requires adjustments to processes and systems and the formalization of standards for performance and conduct.

* A company could go public to raise capital. Such financial arrangements bring constraints and new requirements that can reduce flexibility and require a shift of the corporate culture. Going public requires an increased focus on financial results, a situation that may not align with the desires of those who had joined the business to focus purely on innovation or because its people-first values at the time aligned with their own.

* A company at any stage may upgrade their systems that alter the skills needed to function within the organization.

* Companies may be acquired, or acquire other companies, events that inevitably bring adjustments to processes and systems resulting in transformation to the corporate culture as well.

As discussed in Chapter 7, transparency is critical in times of change and this applies to the evolution of the business. There is often an instinct to avoid talking about the potential impacts of new developments as they could scare employees, but we must resist this instinct. As I've said previously, employees will notice changes. If leaders aren't transparent about them and what they mean, it will create insecurity. It's better to be open that the company's strategies are evolving and adjustments will be needed, but employees will be fully informed and their best interests considered in all decisions.

To keep this promise, leaders need to continually assess the needs of evolving organizations. Through this assessment, they can determine when roles need to change and whether current staff have the competencies to meet the new requirements. I believe that looking out for employees' best interests includes ensuring they're in roles where they can be successful.

To support this strategy, as new leaders are hired, the onboarding process should include a review of the background and competencies of the staff on their team. Employees always have some insecurity when a new boss takes over and I recognize having this unknown person review their résumé could increase that fear. However, I believe it's necessary to ensure that the leader can properly support their team.

If this review is made a formal part of the onboarding process and communicated to employees that it's intended to support them, the transparency and normalcy of the review will reduce fears that an evaluation of their background means they will be let go or that a restructuring is going to occur. The employee should also be involved in the review and given the opportunity to control their own narrative by telling their story. This avoids the insecurity that can be created if people feel they are being discussed behind closed doors. These assessments prevent some of the outcomes outlined in Chapter 9 under "Responsibility Drift."

If an assessment, whether completed during the onboarding of a new leader or as part of the ongoing review of the company's needs, identifies competency gaps between the requirements of a role and the skills of the person currently in the position, then feedback should be given and training and support provided to upgrade the identified competencies.

Ideally, a company's leaders will have developed strong relationships with their teams from the outset. As shared in Chapter

8, with any performance discussions, feedback will be much less threatening if there's trust that the leader wants the most beneficial outcome for the business *and* the employee. If the related leader is new to the organization and thus has not yet developed this relationship with the employee, they should seek the support of HR or another trusted leader in the organization to deliver the feedback to the employee.

Separate from the situation of a new leader, if regular communication between the employee and their leader has already occurred about the evolution of the business and its needs, conversations about changes in the employee's role and the need to upgrade their competencies will be less upsetting since the situation is known.

Particularly in an environment where significant growth is expected, such as in startups, it can save a lot of pain if it's discussed from the beginning, even in the hiring process, that roles will shift as the company's needs evolve and employees will be part of this ongoing discussion.

When an employee's role does change, they will know it and will be aware if they are challenged by the new demands on them. If leaders are transparent and relationships are healthy, the issues can be openly discussed rather than the challenges hidden. This also gives the employee the opportunity to discuss and consider their own feelings about the changes. They are part of the process rather than a victim of it. The reality may be that they don't like the changes in their role or the direction of the business. Through open discussion, all parties can work together to find a resolution.

If, after the effort to discuss the change and upgrade an employee's competencies is made, it's determined an employee is no longer suited to their role, options may be considered to move them to a new position within the organization that better matches their skillset and desired career direction.

Ideally, a position can be found at the same level within the organization, but that isn't often the case. And if it isn't, leaders need to resist the desire to placate by creating a role that awkwardly fits into the corporate structure or placing the employee into a position they also aren't likely to succeed in.

I have seen leaders uncertain what to do with an employee who's no longer a fit for their existing role create a role that isn't truly needed and doesn't align with the overall corporate structure.

For example, after concluding an individual isn't able to manage a team, their direct reports are assigned to a new manager, but the employee maintains their manager title. This occurs even though they no longer have any direct reports and now report to a manager themselves. Despite the change, their name remains on the company's list of managers, so they continue to be invited to all manager meetings and events along with their boss, even though they are no longer a true manager. This kind of situation is awkward for all involved. It's obvious that the leaders couldn't make a tough decision and now employees are left to deal with the consequences.

Any benefit from placating will be short term if it puts someone into a role they aren't suited for or doesn't align with the needs or structure of the business. If the position the employee is most likely to succeed in is at a lower level in the organization, that's what's best for the person, the company, and the broader team. Otherwise, they are likely to become insecure in another role they don't have the necessary skills for or obviously isn't aligned with the corporate structure.

Being offered a demotion can be hard on the psyche, but if after careful consideration, this is determined to be the most effective strategy for the future success of the business and the employee, this difficult decision must be made.

A common scenario, particularly in a startup environment, is in the earlier stage of the company's trajectory, an employee is given a title that doesn't actually align with the level of their experience or the needs of the role. If the business later becomes successful and grows, it may need the skills normally ascribed to this higher-level title. This situation was referred to in Chapter 9 under "Title Misalignment." For example, an employee given a title chief marketing officer (CMO) may be performing at the level of director of marketing and also receiving a director-level salary. If the company is successful, they may get to a stage where they can afford and need a true CMO.

The current CMO would certainly find it difficult to learn someone will be hired above them and their title needs to be lowered. However, if the decision is avoided and the current CMO is left in a role they are no longer the right fit for, they are being set up for failure. And the company will not reach its goals either. It's much better (and kinder, in my opinion) to give the employee the opportunity to move to a position that's a better fit than to allow them to deteriorate in the wrong role.

In the case of the CMO role, where a more experienced person is being brought in above the employee, the benefit of the mentorship and learning from the new leader should be emphasized. Ego may make it difficult to immediately accept this, but if they are able to, they will benefit from the growth that working with an experienced senior executive can provide.

I will restate that this situation can be avoided if appropriate titles that suit the responsibilities and expectations of the role are given from the beginning. It will also be easier to manage if open discussions occur from day one that if the company is successful, roles will shift. This can include being transparent that if a C-level title is given, a reduction of that title may be required if significant growth occurs and the company needs to hire an experienced senior executive. This requires a lot of foresight, but it will make the transition easier if this situation transpires.

Before a proposal is made to move an employee to a lower level, a significantly different role, or change a title, leaders must consult with their HR team and/or legal counsel. In many jurisdictions, a significant change in role could be considered a "constructive dismissal," which has legal implications. It may be necessary to offer a severance package if the change isn't acceptable to the employee. There is also the challenge of salary; if there's consideration to reduce the employee's salary along with the role change, this should be discussed with legal counsel as well.

If another suitable position within the organization isn't available or it's mutually agreed that the working relationship is no longer a fit, a layoff may be required. Leading a business or team requires tough personnel decisions like this, but I'm a strong believer that the right person in the right role is better for everyone (including the employee in the impacted role) and the business.

All exited employees should be treated with respect for their contribution to the company and as outlined in "Face It When You Don't Hire Well," given support to find a new job, but these difficult decisions must be made to ensure the success of the business and its employees.

If we're open and honest about employees' competencies and the potential evolution of the business from the beginning, these situations will be much easier. Changes need to be communicated with empathy and respect, but if we have built a secure trusting relationship with our employees, this can result in better opportunities for all parties in the long run.

WHY THIS MATTERS TO YOU

The Right Role at the Right Time with the Right Support

Identifying the competencies and traits needed for a role and where gaps in these areas can be supported by the business ensures individuals are hired who will be secure in their roles and can excel. This also reduces costly hiring misfires.

The Title Must Fit the Role

An employee who is given a title far above their experience level will likely become insecure when they can't keep up with others at their level. Multiple factors should be considered before selecting or changing someone's title to ensure there aren't negative consequences.

Be Honest about the Good and the Bad with Prospective Hires

If the chosen candidate joins a work environment and finds it's not as advertised, this will create distrust that will be difficult to overcome. If the challenges in an organization are shared with a candidate during the recruitment process, they will join ready to manage those challenges and improve the business.

Introduce New Hires with Strong Onboarding

There is no better time to create comfort and safety in a workplace than when an employee first joins the company. If they become insecure because of poor onboarding, it's difficult to correct.

Face It When You Don't Hire Well

Delaying the termination of a poorly suited hire creates dysfunction for the team and company and wastes time. Also, contrary to how it may feel, it's not kind to delay terminations, as the underperforming employee will likely sense they're not living up to expectations and will become insecure.

Role Evolution

Having the right people in the right roles is an ongoing effort as companies evolve. However, it's in the best interest of the business and employees for leaders to monitor changes in their organization. Training or adjustments may be required to ensure employees are not set up for failure in roles they're no longer a fit for. Not only will this reduce corporate performance, but it will create insecurity in the workforce as well.

CHAPTER 11

THE IMPACT OF TOXIC LEADERSHIP BEHAVIOR

*"You cannot manage other people unless
you manage yourself first."*

—Peter Drucker

As leaders, we typically direct the work of many people within a company, or if we're a CEO or president, we set the tone for the whole organization. Employees look to us for the behaviors that are accepted and valued.

As a result, when leaders display toxic conduct, this has greater negative impact than when a nonleader behaves the same way.

Research has shown that abusive behavior by leaders can spread throughout companies. When leaders act in a harmful way, employees model the conduct; through observation, they conclude that such behavior is acceptable, and this results in a culture of abuse

(Priesemuth 2020). Other studies support this observation, finding that employees who experience abuse from a boss are more likely to treat others in the same manner, causing a ripple effect of interpersonal damage through the company (Priesemuth 2020).

I have personally seen and felt the impact that toxic leadership conduct has on an organization. I have also heard many stories from people whose careers and personal lives have been significantly disrupted by a boss's behavior. I will share some of these stories in this chapter.

These stories paint a distressing picture, but unfortunately, such toxicity is all too common in workplaces, and the impacts are far too significant to ignore. I would love to tell you that these occurrences are rare, but unfortunately, most of us will work with or under a leader displaying toxic behaviors at some point in our career.

In fairness, leaders like all individuals are products of their environment. Any toxic conduct is learned either from our own leaders or adults earlier in our lives or we're using protective behaviors due to our own insecurities or challenges. I have empathy for all who have suffered, but it doesn't excuse the poor treatment of others.

LEADING WITH FEAR

Throughout my career, I have seen old-school leaders use fear tactics to control and motivate their teams. They seem to believe that instilling fear in subordinates is necessary to get results. I don't agree, and neither do most leadership experts today. However, I've also seen insecure leaders use fear to control their employees. It's as if in their own state of fear, they don't realize they are capable of motivating their teams any other way.

This next story is an example of an insecure leader who used fear to control his teams.

Joe had been the chief technology officer (CTO) at Company V for over five years. He'd joined the organization fifteen years earlier as an IT analyst right after completing his two-year college business degree. He learned on the job and learned well, but his lack of outside experience and relatively low level of education compared to CTOs in other companies gave Joe an inferiority complex. It weighed on him that most of his peers held bachelor's degrees or MBAs, not two-year college degrees.

He took his feelings of inferiority out on his subordinates. In his team meetings, Joe would make comments "in jest" but really with the intention of instilling fear. Example: When an employee was leaving the company, Joe said that they were lucky they were leaving on good terms. He claimed that he knew a lot of people, and if anyone left on bad terms, he could ruin them professionally. Then he laughed.

Joe had a long history of using passive-aggressive behavior and fear tactics with his team, so they knew the comment wasn't a joke. They all laughed nervously, but the tension in the room was palpable.

Joe also constantly gave painful negative feedback to his direct reports and told them that they needed to learn to "take it." Joe drilled the belief into them that he knew better in all situations. As a result, his direct reports were filled with self-doubt and insecurity in addition to their fear of him.

Joe maintained control and propped up his own ego with these behaviors. In doing so, he created a dysfunctional environment

> where nothing happened unless he dictated it, and employees
> tiptoed around him in fear. As a result, the company was slow to
> evolve and grew at a much slower pace than competitors.

Both passive and direct fear-inducing conduct by leaders create a toxic work environment.

Passive-aggressive fear tactics are confusing and stressful for employees. They may wonder if they've misunderstood the intent of the words, or if the leader does mean to scare them. They can never quite be certain where they stand.

In contrast, Joe's constant negative feedback to his direct reports kept them in a weakened state, fearful of doing anything that would bring them further psychological harm.

Although, it's true that fear can motivate, it does so in a negative way, driving someone to take action to avoid an unpleasant situation rather than empowering them to tackle a challenge on their own initiative. An employee may do what a bullying leader says, but the actions will be motivated by fear rather than inspiration. When we aren't truly inspired to do something, it will not be our best effort.

I've even seen motivating with fear have the opposite of its intended effect by causing employees to freeze; they become incapable of getting their work done because they're consumed with anxiety about a potential backlash from their boss. In that situation, even subpar performance isn't achieved.

In addition to being a poor motivator, leading with fear has other negative consequences. A 2018 study found that leaders who control through fear end up stifling their staff's creativity and initiative (Guo et al. 2018). You'll recall how fear triggers the fight-or-flight response, leading to lower quality and quantity of work.

Yet, I still hear arguments there is a place for fear in business. Certainly, I will concede that being afraid of letting someone down could be motivational. However, the motivating factor can't be fear of being bullied or demeaned. Not wanting to disappoint a customer could be motivational, but being terrified that if we "disappoint" our boss we will be publicly shamed can be paralyzing.

Demeaning and Bullying

"There's a big difference between being demanding and being demeaning. Great leaders don't undermine people—they elevate them."

—ADAM GRANT (@ADAMMGRANT, AUGUST 3, 2018)

Demeaning others is a common toxic behavior that instills fear. It's often used to make the abuser feel superior and prop up their psyche. Demeaning is also a form of bullying and can rise to the level of contravening workplace safety legislation.

Bill, in this next story, was new in his position as CEO. He lacked experience managing multidisciplined teams, so he resorted to bullying tactics in an attempt to show dominance.

> Bill participated in a conference call in which a cross-functional team was reviewing a draft proposal for a customer. In this organization, proposals were a group effort due to the complexity of the product and pricing. The team was discussing comments and edits that had been inserted into the proposal by the salesperson responsible for the deal.

> Bill used this as an opportunity to assert dominance. He asked why the salesperson would edit a document that should be owned by the marketing department. He declared that the marketing department should be the only ones making changes to proposals and that this was an amateur way to manage a critical tender.
>
> Raising the heat, he asked who was responsible for the document. Julia, the marketing manager, cautiously spoke up and said that she was managing the proposal. Bill told her the process was dysfunctional and she shouldn't allow anyone other than herself to edit the document. He then laid down the law, saying it would not be handled this way in the future.

Bill failed to have a simple private discussion with Julia beforehand to learn about the process and the rationale for it, yet he publicly rejected it, demanded changes, and called out the actions of the salesperson. These demeaning actions put the entire team on the defensive and into self-protection mode for future conversations and meetings with this leader. They now knew they would be called out publicly for any actions he deemed out of line.

Weak or inexperienced leaders like Bill may try to control their staff by demeaning and bullying them. This behavior embarrasses and shames the employees, damaging their self-esteem and their perceived esteem in the eyes of others. It can also cause them to head for the exits as soon as they find a job elsewhere.

A bullying boss may also use subtle comments that could almost be unnoticeable to a bystander but slowly eat away at the confidence of employees they're aimed at. For example, they may intentionally show great surprise that a subordinate figured something out and say something like, "I didn't think you'd get that, given your lack of technical knowledge." Or they may ask people to explain things in simpler terms for an employee as way of demeaning them. These are verbal humiliations and putdowns that you can't quite put your finger on but create self-doubt and shame. These abuses accumulate day after day, increasing the targeted employee's insecurity.

As an alternative tactic, a toxic leader may directly point out all an employee's errors, no matter how small, reprimand them in public and in private, and accompany the callout with highly critical and often undeserved personal negative feedback. They may defend their conduct by saying, "At least you know where you stand with me." But we all need to understand that there is *no* circumstance under which bullying behaviors are fair, warranted, professional, or acceptable in the workplace.

Furthermore, the results will be negative. Underachieving employees should be performance managed. The performance management may ultimately result in termination, but it should never involve psychological abuse.

The creation of insecurity caused by this abuse will only result in the behaviors described in Chapters 3 and 4 and make it impossible for the employee to improve their performance. Resources, both in time and money, will be wasted and the tasks assigned to the person completed poorly until they either decide to leave or are let go.

Not only is demeaning and bullying conduct by leaders unethical, but it also costs businesses real money. The behavior will result in higher staff turnover, less favorable attitudes about jobs and the company, and greater psychological distress than in a nonbullying environment (Tepper 2000). We need to stop allowing bullies to damage our people and the performance of our businesses.

MICROMANAGING

"Micromanaging and protecting one's territory
are about guarding one's own ego and absolute belief in
being right above and beyond all others."

—Mitchell Kusy and Elizabeth Holloway

Many of us, particularly when we are new leaders, may feel nervous about delegating tasks. It can be nerve wracking to trust others with important jobs, but it's also necessary to be successful. Controlling every task is inefficient, and micromanagement can be toxic to the employee experiencing it from their boss, disempowering them and creating deep insecurity. Yet, despite these negatives, micromanagement is very common.

Management reaches a toxic level when leaders closely monitor their employees' work to an extent that is far beyond what's reasonable to ensure that tasks get done. Micromanagers constantly remind their staff about tasks and highlight any deficiencies, no matter how minute.

Micromanagers typically require employees to perform their work exactly as they themselves would, even when there are multiple ways to achieve the same results. If the staff don't use the manager's approach, the results are rejected as not good enough, even if the outcomes are correct and according to specifications. Micromanagement stifles creativity and innovation because it permits no deviation from the method the manager prescribes.

This next story is of a micromanaging leader, Ian, who couldn't resist controlling the work of Joseph who moved into a role he had previously held.

Joseph was promoted into the role of product manager. He'd been working on the product team for a few years and was ready for the role. He knew the product and the company's processes well. He reported to Ian, the director of product. Ian had previously managed the same product. Joseph was excited to have Ian as his leader. He could learn a lot from him.

However, what he found instead was that Ian wanted to direct all of his work. In their one-to-ones, Joseph tried to raise novel strategies to manage the product, but Ian would respond with his own directives and no discussion of Joseph's ideas.

Since Joseph was ultimately responsible for the success of the product, he tried a few new strategies without consulting Ian first. This was within his mandate. When Ian found out, he asked Joseph not to take actions again without consulting him beforehand. After that incident, Ian began checking with Joseph multiple times a day, asking what he was working on and whether he had completed the tasks they had talked about.

He asked Joseph to cc him on all discussions with the product's sales team. It was extremely frustrating for Joseph since he already had relationships with the sales team from his previous role. Now someone was monitoring all of his interactions with them. It was embarrassing.

Ian had repeatedly inserted himself into email discussions to raise additional points or "clarify" something that Joseph had said. These were often points that Joseph had been waiting to bring up until later in the sales cycle, but Ian was forcing issues earlier, unnecessarily so in Joseph's mind.

Joseph felt completely untrusted. It was confusing as the product was doing very well. Joseph was having success with the tasks he was allowed to do. Yet, with Ian watching his work so closely, he didn't feel like he was the manager of the product at all. His motivation lagged. Any effort seemed pointless since Ian would likely come in and change, or minimize, the efforts he'd made. No matter how small the issue, Ian had something to say about it.

Demonstrating the epitome of micromanaging, Ian was getting involved in even the most minute aspects of Joseph's work. I've seen micromanagers try and justify this type of behavior by saying, "If I don't know I can trust you with the small things, how can I know I can trust you with the big things?" However, the conduct is often about the leader's own mental state and their need to control, not the employee's work.

Micromanagement is frequently combined with demeaning and bullying behavior. This next story describes such a situation faced by Erin.

Erin, a well-respected sales leader, was preparing a proposal for a new customer. Erin made an estimate of the appropriate product pricing and obtained approval from her boss, Jim.

She later shared the proposal with the vice-president of product, Aidan, who informed Erin that the pricing was too low for the version of the product this customer needed. Aidan requested that Erin slightly increase the pricing to ensure costs were fully covered. Erin agreed since Aidan was far more experienced in the product line than she or Jim and the impact was minimal.

Erin made the change in the proposal and sent it back to Jim for final approval. Upon reviewing the pricing change, he became enraged and called her unprofessional. He stated that she was not acting as a sales leader should and that she had handled the situation extremely poorly.

Jim said this over text message, without having a conversation with Erin to understand why she'd made the pricing change. He simply couldn't handle that she would seek advice from someone else and therefore diminish his control over the situation, even though Aidan was an authority on the product line, not to mention in a superior leadership position.

Jim's text tirade left Erin in tears. It was unacceptable treatment of any human being, even if they had made a mistake. Erin left the company shortly thereafter.

Jim was an unstable leader who micromanaged to retain control and was easily triggered to bullying tactics to assert dominance. The result wasn't only hard on Erin, who shouldn't have had to deal with such conduct, but the organization also lost an employee. The business had to incur the costs of recruitment, manage the effort to onboard and train a new hire, and explain the departure of a well-respected team member.

The abusive, out-of-control behavior that Jim displayed would make anyone afraid to make decisions themselves or take actions without consulting their boss. An employee treated this way will rapidly become insecure about the quality of their work, even if they've had a history of successes under other managers. Those who are confident in their abilities will likely leave an organization that allows micromanagement to persist.

In addition to being unkind and unprofessional, this leadership style is also out of pace with the values of many current work environments in which employees expect autonomy and flexibility, along with collegial respect. Micromanagement and extreme command-and-control approaches aren't acceptable in today's business world.

JEKYLL AND HYDE

Stories like this next one about Ted, whose erratic moods created a toxic work environment, are all too common. I've experienced multiple leaders like this myself and heard many stories of leaders whose moods would swing without warning and who didn't seem to realize the impact their conduct had on those around them.

In her HR role, Marissa worked closely with Ted. Ted was a team leader who was known for being a "cool guy" to go out for a beer with. He was often jovial and liked to have a good time. But he was also known for lashing out viciously when he was in a bad mood or felt threatened.

On one occasion, Marissa was supporting Ted's recruitment of a software developer and brought him a résumé to review. She told him she thought the candidate was a great fit. Ted snapped at her, "And how could you possibly know if a developer is a great fit? You have no technical skills."

Marissa felt stung by the hostility of the comment since just an hour earlier, they'd eaten a friendly lunch together. She was completely unprepared for the hurtful remark. She went back to her office and shed a few tears.

Ted's job was high intensity and he also had a busy family life. The pressure of those responsibilities caused him to become reactive and toxic.

New employees got an initial impression that this was a great guy and that he'd be fun to work with. Then they stepped the wrong way and were destroyed by his words. Although Ted was nice 80 percent of the time, the fear of psychological harm from him the other 20 percent of the time caused everyone to walk on eggshells around him, afraid to set him off.

This made Ted's workforce extremely dysfunctional. His team was insecure and fearful of making any moves that could trigger him, radically slowing the department's progress in meeting its objectives. People avoided interacting with Ted's department in general; many of them had seen Ted's bad side and didn't want to experience it again.

Ted's view of himself likely focused in tightly on the 80 percent of the time that he was a "cool guy" without acknowledging the other 20 percent and the deeply negative impact that his erratic, hostile behavior had on the team.

Unfortunately, I've become an expert on this topic, having worked with many unpredictable leaders. I have seen valued employees leave, poor performance increase, and mental health deteriorate under bosses who are unstable and unpredictable like Ted.

In the worst cases, these leaders inflict extreme "Jekyll and Hyde" type conduct on their staff. They seem to have difficulty controlling their emotions, swinging from one extreme position to another rapidly and unexpectedly. They also experience emotions strongly. For example, they may be calmly reviewing someone's work until they see a small mistake and are triggered into a rage.

I had one leader who often expressed genuine care about my success and demonstrated values that I believe in. But then at completely unexpected times, they would lash out with a hurtful comment or express enormous rage over something I had done that hadn't met their often-unspoken expectations. At other times, they would have no reactions at all to errors that I thought deserved a reprimand. The interactions mimicked a classic abusive relationship pattern in which the perpetrator manipulates the victim by giving them the support they need when the perpetrator's in a good mood but lashes out at them when not.

This type of erratic behavior is extremely stressful for employees, as they must always be on guard with the toxic boss. Although my leader's good moods were more prevalent than his bad ones, the unpredictability of the negative outbursts left me on edge, never knowing when I would be verbally assaulted next. It greatly reduced my ability to focus on my work because I was always watchful for signs of a bad mood and cautious not to trigger a negative reaction.

I have observed that this "Jekyll and Hyde" behavior is prevalent in insecure leaders. John Maxwell, a famous leadership expert, supports this view with his statement, "Insecure leaders are like fireworks with a lit fuse. It's only a matter of time until they explode, and when they do, they hurt everyone close to them" (The John Maxwell Company 2014).

UNTRUSTWORTHY
LEADERS

It's not only the obviously toxic leaders who create insecurity in employees. In this next story, Brad didn't demean or micromanage anyone on his team, yet he still lost their trust and contributed to a toxic environment.

Brad had been in the head of sales role at Company E for two years when he was asked to take on marketing as well. His new role would be senior vice-president, sales and marketing. This required replacing himself in the head of sales position.

Brad was nervous about the promotion because he hadn't run Marketing before. He wanted someone in the head of sales position whom he could rely on and control.

An old colleague, Kelsey, was available. Brad knew Kelsey could be difficult to work with and used fear to control her teams, but he also knew that she was both skilled and, more importantly, would do everything that he asked. Brad convinced himself that he could mitigate the impacts of Kelsey's toxic management style. He felt that it would be worth the effort since he would be less stressed knowing that someone he trusted was leading the sales department.

Kelsey joined the company and immediately asserted dominance by bullying and micromanaging the sales team. Brad was so caught up in learning his new responsibilities that he couldn't oversee Kelsey as he had convinced himself that he would.

Now forced to work in a toxic environment, the staff quickly lost trust in Brad. They knew he had worked with Kelsey before and was aware of her bullying, yet hired her and allowed her to behave in her accustomed fashion. The team saw that to improve his personal situation, Brad had risked their mental health by recruiting Kelsey.

Once trust in Brad's judgment was gone, it was impossible for the employees to believe the situation could improve. Three high-performing sales managers left the business within five months of Kelsey taking over the role. They wouldn't work under a bully. When better opportunities came up, they took them.

In Brad's nepotistic hiring of Kelsey, he may not have exhibited toxic conduct himself but accepting those behaviors in her rendered him untrustworthy to his staff. A hallmark of trustworthy leaders is their consideration of the business, the employees, and of simply what is right before they consider the impact on themselves. Brad failed to do this.

Leaders who fail to create and maintain trusting relationships with their teams can be as damaging to a corporate culture as those who display overtly toxic conduct. If employees don't trust their boss or their company's top leaders, it will create insecurity since they cannot be certain the leaders will do what's best for the company or them.

Although changes and decisions can have negative consequences, harmful outcomes can often be avoided or the impact reduced when due consideration is made. Employees will see when this consideration wasn't part of a leader's process, and they were not a priority in the decision making.

When a team concludes that they cannot trust their leaders, it shatters the psychological safety of the workplace, makes it unlikely that those employees will buy into any changes the mistrusted leaders put forward. That resistance will greatly reduce the chance that the changes will be successful.

HOW DO TOXIC LEADERS GET INTO THEIR POSITIONS?

It may cross your mind that an easy way to avoid toxic leadership is not to hire employees that display toxic behavior to begin with. However, it isn't always that straightforward. A leader who demeans and bullies their team could be placed in a leadership position if the hiring manager doesn't know their character well, or a person could only begin displaying toxic conduct after they assume the role.

Unfortunately, the promotion of those who use toxic behavior can also go through even with the hiring manager's prior knowledge of their dysfunctional conduct. The reason is that in some toxic corporate environments, harmful behavior is tolerated so long as the perpetrators are "productive." This aligns with the discussion of toxic coworkers in Chapter 5 where it was noted that productivity can be an excuse to allow unacceptable conduct to continue. The conduct will be minimized: "That's just the way they are" or "They mean well but aren't great communicators." Those with the power to intervene instead look away and expect employees to work around the toxicity because that individual has a skill the company needs.

Or perhaps the leader has been with the organization for a long time, so people get used to the behavior even though it's damaging. Research has found that there's a desire for stability within a system that makes people strive to keep things the same, even when they are toxic (Kusy and Holloway 2009). This inertia within a company may allow a bully to remain and even be promoted.

Nepotism can also be the cause of recruiting a toxic leader into an organization or giving someone a promotion despite a known history of damaging conduct. Unfortunately, some people will prefer to work with someone who is a friend and thus a known quantity rather than hire an unknown person, regardless of how ugly and damaging the friend's workplace behavior is known to be. As with Brad's motivation for hiring Kelsey despite her history of bullying, the individual is usually someone who will carry forward the promoter's agenda and broadens their power because they can trust this person to do their bidding.

There's also the very real issue that we can be too quick to make excuses for the harmful conduct. As I shared in the discussion of defense mechanisms, I rationalized the behavior of a bullying boss to make the situation tolerable. I told myself I was being oversensitive or that I misunderstood their intentions.

Many of us have also forgiven our bosses for their hurtful treatment of us, especially if they make amends afterward. I'm guilty of this myself, having made excuses for a boss berating me because "they had a lot on their plate," or "they were having a difficult time at home," or because they seemed to truly feel bad about it.

But the truth is, their effort to make up for bad behavior may simply be manipulation to avoid consequences and not actually having to change their conduct. The actions are rarely new, even if they haven't happened to you before. The perpetrator often knows what they're doing and what actions to take to minimize harm to themselves. Forgiving or rationalizing the behavior only gives the bully license to continue the mistreatment of you or someone else.

We must ask ourselves, is the productivity of a toxic leader worth the consequences of their impact on the broader organization? I strongly believe the answer to this question is no.

One survey found that 44 percent of employees have left a job because of a bad boss (Carucci 2018). Given that staff turnover costs are between 1.5 and 2.5 times the salary paid for the position (Cascio 2015), a toxic leader would have to be *extremely* productive to make up for the costs to the company due to the turnover they leave in their wake.

Toxic Leaders

Toxic leadership behavior has a significant negative effect on the psychological safety in the workplace. The conduct of a leader can spread across the organization since leaders model behavior for employees. Staff may come to believe the toxic conduct is acceptable.

Leading with Fear

Although leading with fear can motivate, it doesn't empower employees. It won't inspire best efforts. Fear can also freeze people, reducing their creativity and productivity.

Demeaning and Bullying

Bullying contravenes workplace safety legislation and can create liability for the business. The behavior can also reduce employees' commitment to the organization, damage mental health, lower productivity, and create a psychologically unsafe work environment.

Micromanagement

Micromanagement will limit the autonomy and lead to those who want to learn and grow leaving the organization. Employees will become insecure about all of their work and afraid to take actions without the agreement of their leaders. This will stunt creativity and innovation.

Jekyll and Hyde

A leader who displays erratic, unpredictable moods can be extremely stressful for employees as they can never be sure of the mood the person is in. This can increase insecurity and harm the productivity of all those impacted by the behavior.

Untrustworthy Leaders

A lack of trust in leadership can make employees insecure as they don't believe their best interests will be considered in decision making. Staff will also be less likely to buy into any changes put forward by an untrusted leader, which will reduce the success of company initiatives.

CHAPTER 12

STRATEGIES TO CULTIVATE PSYCHOLOGICALLY HEALTHY LEADERSHIP

*"But if you ask followers what they need from leaders,
the clear answer is trust, compassion,
stability, and hope."*

—Tom Rath and Barry Conchie (quoted in Robison 2009)

The behaviors in the troubling stories in Chapter 11 don't happen in every organization. Some companies that I've worked at have ingrained healthy values in their cultures, and toxic conduct isn't tolerated. However, harmful behavior is still far too common. Every single person I spoke to while writing this book had a scarring experience with a toxic leader to share. Those scars run deep and can stay with us for our whole careers.

We must reduce the number of people who endure these emotional injuries by consciously taking actions to stop this damaging conduct. This chapter describes ways a company can select and develop quality leaders while also ensuring a channel is available so that employees can safely report incidents of toxic behavior.

I will also refer back to the section in Chapter 6 on "Dealing with Harmful Behaviors." If you do have a leader in your organization who is exhibiting the conduct discussed in the previous chapter, it's critical that you address this and not allow it to continue. The solutions in this chapter can help your business avoid being in that situation, but if this behavior is present, it must be addressed to stop the harm to the employees in your company.

ASSESS VALUES ALIGNMENT IN THE LEADERSHIP RECRUITMENT PROCESS

The hiring principles outlined in Chapter 10 apply to leaders too. However, as discovered by Company N in this next story, values alignment takes an even greater importance in the recruitment of those who will direct teams.

> Company N had recently parted ways with their director of sales, who had been in the role for a year. Although that individual had the right product knowledge and sales skills, their values hadn't fit into Company N's culture.
>
> The former director had believed that oversight, bordering on micromanagement, was needed to motivate the sales team.

But Company N was a fast-moving casual startup that valued autonomy and trust. The misalignment made it difficult for functional working relationships to form, and the resulting inefficiencies caused sales to stagnate.

John, VP of Sales, learned from this experience and prioritized an alignment in values in the recruitment of the new director. To avoid the personal biases that can influence an interview process, John had the top candidates write a summary of their leadership style.

He asked them to include the key lessons learned throughout their career and the accomplishment they were most proud of. The aspects of their journeys that the candidates chose to share quickly highlighted the right choice.

Quinn wrote that her leadership style was to empower her team by trusting them to do their jobs. However, she would always be available for support and aware of their progress. She gave continuous feedback and promoted professional growth.

Quinn shared that what she'd learned about leadership was the importance of "walking the talk." She realized her actions must match her words and that to maintain the trust of her team, any deviations needed to be explained.

She said her moment of greatest pride was when her team reached a sales goal many had thought unachievable. She wrote that this pride was not just in herself but in the recognition given to her team members, who had stretched themselves to reach the target. They were proud of their accomplishment, and she was proud of them.

Quinn didn't have the level of product knowledge that the previous director of sales had possessed, but John felt she could learn. He believed the team would rally around the right leader and support them to get up to speed on the product.

John was right. Quinn joined the team and quickly gained the trust of her employees with her authentic demeanor and obvious desire for their success. A year into the role, the sales team beat the prior year's targets and were working together in a way John had never seen before. Prioritizing values over product knowledge had paid off.

John's method of asking candidates to write an essay is an effective way to identify and easily compare each person's leadership approach. However, not all candidates will be skilled writers, so depending on the role, this may not be the most appropriate assessment method. Alternatively, interviews can be used to systematically uncover the candidates' traits that are central to the culture of the organization.

Regardless of the approach, the goal of the selection process is to look beyond what's visible on the candidate's résumé. The résumé may get a candidate to the table, but the process must assess who the candidate really is and whether they align with the company's values.

I put a lot of focus on values in my recruitment of leaders because I strongly believe in the importance of values alignment. I approach the interviews casually to allow genuine conversation to flow. However, I also target specific areas (which I list below) to get a sense of what's important to the individual and what aspects of their prior roles have had the greatest impact on them.

If a candidate mentions only their financial or process improvement accomplishments, rather than the achievements of their teams, it's a sign that our values may not be aligned. If I were asked about the outcomes from my past leadership roles that I take the most pride in, I would provide examples of when I supported my teams to achieve high performance and to empower their professional growth. These accomplishments naturally led to outstanding financial and efficiency results.

Here are questions to consider to develop a profile of leadership candidates:

- **What is one of your biggest career successes?** It's a good sign if the candidate mentions the contribution of others and shares credit for the success.
- **Share a career failure that had a significant impact on you. How did the failure occur?** The ideal response will convey humility about the failure and not place blame on others or external factors.
- **Provide an example of raising a problem with a superior.** If the company desires an environment where employees are safe to speak their minds, the identification of leaders who will demonstrate this behavior is important.
- **What have you done to support your own growth, both professionally and personally?** The answer will ascertain whether the candidate's approach aligns with the company's prioritization of learning.
- **Provide an example of constructive feedback you've received and what you did with the feedback.** This will demonstrate whether the candidate is comfortable sharing areas in which they currently need, or have needed, improvement and can reveal their vulnerability.

- **What is your leadership style?** This must align with the company's values. The answer should be validated through references from a former leader and a subordinate to confirm that the style outlined by the candidate is what they exhibited in the workplace.
- **Provide an example of a time that you led through a crisis.** The ideal answer will demonstrate that they reacted quickly in a crisis situation and didn't freeze or avoid the challenge.
- **Provide the profile of your direct reports from a recent leadership role. How did you support their growth?** The question will provide evidence of whether they're comfortable leading and growing a high-performing team.

The questions are beneficial for the recruitment of leaders, but the first five questions can also be used in interviewing candidates for other roles. It's crucial to ensure that those who represent a company set the right tone with the values they promote.

PROVIDE LEADERS
WITH EXECUTIVE COACHING

The use of executive coaches has become more prevalent in organizations today, but I don't believe the value of coaching is fully recognized in the corporate world yet.

To shed some light on the benefits of coaching, I asked a friend of mine, Mike Watson, Founder and Principal of Ignite Management Services and an executive coach, for a client success story. His response inspired me more than I'd expected. It also aligns with what I've presented throughout this book.

Mike's client, Kelly, was the CEO of a company she founded. This company was now struggling with negativity in its corporate culture. Mike entered the situation as not just a coach; he also performed a situational assessment. This involved one-to-one interviews with many members of Kelly's team.

When the interviews were complete, he sat down for a coaching session with Kelly and said, "This is a tough conversation for me...because I know you, I respect you, and I know you to be a caring person. But for a number of reasons, your staff don't see you that way. They are intimidated by you, and they feel that you will stomp on them if they make mistakes."

No one else had been able to give Kelly this feedback. However, when Mike did without any bias or skin in the game, Kelly took it on and a significant turnaround resulted.

Often, bringing in an external person, like Mike, not just for coaching but also to assess the situation, can reveal a leader's blind spots, creating an opportunity for growth that would be unlikely without intervention.

Yet, it's not always easy to show the ROI of coaching. The obvious result in Mike's story isn't the standard outcome; although effective, the impact is usually more subtle. Therefore, an advocate within an organization is often needed to promote the benefits of coaching.

In my experience, companies engage executive coaches when someone on the leadership team has had a positive experience with coaching. They see the value and share it with the rest of the organization. Or sometimes someone in the HR department is trained as a coach and demonstrates the value of the skill and advocates for it within the business.

I was fortunate to work at an organization that had a number of coaches on its people team. This is where I became a big supporter of coaching. Prior to this experience, I was successful, but I still lacked confidence. I hadn't taken a step back to process my accomplishments.

The coaches helped me slow down, breathe, and really look at my career progression. That helped me build the confidence to make tough decisions and trust my instincts. My career continued to excel as I became bolder in sharing my opinions and in pushing initiatives forward. I believe that if more leaders experience effective coaching, the recognition of its value will grow, and its prevalence will increase.

So what can a coach do for you and/or the leaders on your team? For starters, they play a different role than that of a therapist, focusing on the future rather than the past. The coach acts as an external supplier of candor, providing leaders with the impartial feedback needed for growth. From my own experience and that of those I've spoken to, if the "coachee" (the person being coached) is engaged and participates wholeheartedly in the coaching, it can bring the following benefits:

- **Increased self-awareness.** The coach pushes the coachee to understand the motivation of certain behaviors or actions. This process can reduce the use of defense mechanisms and bias. It can also increase personal growth because the coachee attains a better understanding of themselves. Through this understanding, the coachees can see their impact on others more clearly, as well as see the reaction of others to them. This can be helpful if a leader is unknowingly exhibiting the "Jekyll and Hyde" behavior described in Chapter 11.

- **Improved ability to control emotions.** Once we're aware of our emotions and what's driving them, we can step back when we get a familiar rush of feelings and think about whether it's useful. This can help leaders who have angry outbursts or lack patience. This can also reduce the chance of "Jekyll and Hyde" behavior.

- **Increased empathy.** As our understanding of our own emotions and reactions increases, it can create awareness and understanding of the emotions of others. In learning about our own triggers, we come to understand that others have the same mechanisms and become more sympathetic and less reactive to them. This can help those leaders who are using fear to lead to understand the impact it has on employees.

One caution with coaching is that it may be most beneficial to help high-potential and good leaders become great leaders, rather than reform toxic leaders. The authors of the book *Toxic Workplace!* found that toxic leaders have an "unwillingness or inability to acknowledge the inappropriateness of their behavior. This makes it unlikely that coaching strategies, focusing on feedback and change, would be easily accepted" (Kusy and Holloway 2009, 1018). This presumption won't apply in every case, as I believe many people simply aren't aware of the impact of their conduct, so increasing their awareness and empathy would be helpful. However, the finding is worthy of consideration and for setting expectations if you attempt to improve a toxic leader's behavior through coaching.

Of course, another challenge is finding quality coaches. Coaching is an unregulated field, and like any field of this nature, anyone can call themselves a coach. However, if you rely on references and your network, you will certainly find excellent coaches to assist you.

ENGAGE TRAINED FACILITATORS FOR SIGNIFICANT LEADERSHIP MEETINGS

Leadership meetings are opportunities to build secure relationships among peers and ensure that teams are aligned. However, meetings often don't achieve the desired results and simply waste time. This next story about Company I shows how engaging a facilitator can improve the communication among team members and thus the outcome of a meeting.

> Company I's leadership team was new to working together. The CEO, Leanne, had joined the organization only six months earlier. Three other members of the eight-person team had joined within the past four months.
>
> Although the team had begun to form positive working relationships, they were still learning about one another. Leanne felt this was the right time to bring in a facilitator to run a one-day leadership meeting to deepen the connections and open up communication.
>
> Scott was hired to run the session. He was given the mandate to create an environment in which the attendees would feel safe to speak their minds. Before the meeting, he asked each person to send him a photo of something that was important to them

that they were open to talking about at the session.

He started the day with the photos as an icebreaker, asking each person to explain the image and what it meant to them. You could see the nervousness in the room diminish as each person talked about something that gave them positive emotions.

Scott took advantage of the openness and moved to the next part of the agenda where he asked the team members to each share a factor they felt was stunting the business's growth or limiting the team's success.

"Lack of experience," "inconsistent data," and "too many goals" were all thrown out.

The group took each topic and dived into its meaning and each person's view on it. Scott gave Leanne the opportunity to speak on each topic. Leanne zeroed in on "lack of experience" since this was raised by Max, who'd been with the company for ten years.

Scott facilitated a discussion between Leanne and Max about his concern that Leanne and the other new members of the team wouldn't learn the business fast enough to capitalize on current opportunities. Leanne admitted she would need the support of each team member to help her and the new leaders learn the intricacies of the organization.

Scott took this moment to ask each person whether they would provide this support. They all agreed that they would. This was a critical point in the session.

The meeting went on to discuss strategy points and next steps, but those initial few hours of the session created a platform for the team to work from in the future. All the attendees did support Leanne and the rest of the team to learn the business. Leanne successfully led the company to their highest sales year ever.

With Scott's help, the outcome of Company I's meeting was exceptional. Most meetings don't come near that level of success for these reasons:

- If the person steering the meeting is the leader of the organization or team, employees may go into listening mode rather than contributing to the discussion. This can happen even if attendees are specifically asked to contribute.
- If the person running the meeting has a particular bias, they may guide the discussion by creating room for people who support them to speak and not for those who don't. This may be an unconscious action by the meeting leader but regardless has the effect of stunting the conversation.
- Some team members may be faster to speak up than others, which may not allow time for those who take longer to process their thoughts to share their views.

However, with intention, meetings can be effective. Though, in my experience, it's rare for an internal team to improve dysfunctional meeting habits on their own.

Engaging a facilitator like Scott can greatly improve the functioning of meetings. The facilitator essentially acts like the head of an orchestra, ensuring that goals are clear and everyone knows their part. We saw Scott take advantage of the right time to make connections and ask the team to dive deeper into topics.

The facilitator will also do the following:

- Keep the meeting on track and on time.

- Ensure that no one dominates the meeting and all voices are heard.
- Work, in a constructive way, to defuse any tensions or conflicts that arise. We saw this when Scott created space for Leanne and Max to address the difficult topic of "lack of experience" without negativity.
- Ensure that ideas and actions are captured, and everyone walks away from the meeting understanding expectations and next steps.

This all sounds amazing, so why wouldn't we want this for all meetings?

Although facilitators are effective, they can be expensive. I don't think a facilitator is needed for every meeting, but it's definitely worth considering them for important sessions, such as during strategy development or when a team has a history of dysfunctional meetings that don't achieve objectives.

My recommendation is to use skilled facilitators for critical meetings and train people on the team, but not the boss or team leader, to fulfill the role for sessions of lower importance.

TEAM BUILDING
FOR COMPANY LEADERSHIP

The highest-performing leadership teams that I've been part of have been those in which each leader truly supported the others' successes. But it takes effort and intention to establish these powerful connections among peers, especially when teams are geographically dispersed.

I've personally seen and felt the strength of leadership teams grow when the following methods are used to establish openness and positivity in the relationships across the organization.

- **Leadership retreats.** Leadership retreats give employees unique shared experiences that can accelerate bonding. They are also opportunities for training on topics that are crucial to the business and for leaders to come together to discuss and inspire one another around the company's mission and vision.

- **Leadership pairs or triads.** Creating pairs or triads of leaders who coach one another and share on a regular basis provides a useful way to build relationships, provide support, and allow participants to hone their coaching skills. Hearing the challenges of peers can also reduce the insecurity that we feel when we think we're the only one facing issues.

- **Promoting interdepartmental leadership interaction.** Information should be shared regularly rather than only when issues arise. The forum for this could be regular meetings or events, but for efficiency, chat groups and department newsletters are also helpful. This will avoid communication silos.

- **Sharing each leader's skillset and experiences.** Ensuring that leaders are aware of the experience and skills of their peers will increase collaboration. If leaders know their peers have experience in particular areas, they can engage with those peers when their insight is needed. This can be achieved by profiling leaders when they join the company and maintaining these profiles in a location accessible to all.

Natural human connections and great chemistry can create spontaneous bonds, but companies can foster these connections or speed them up by taking these and similar actions.

PROVIDE TRAINING TO EXISTING AND UPCOMING LEADERS

Even if you excel at identifying and recruiting strong leaders, every recruit will have an area that can be improved through training to help them grow and perform optimally. Aspiring leaders within an organization will also benefit from training to develop into healthy leaders.

Company S in this next story believed in the power of leadership training.

Company S held annual cross-functional leadership retreats that brought all members of its senior and executive teams together for training and team building. The retreats were intended to build relationships between leaders and provide education on topics that were important to the business. Sessions covered subjects such as overviews of company policies (including appropriate workplace behaviors), management skills, corporate values, and general industry matters that support the efficiency of the organization.

The retreats were an excellent opportunity for the leaders to learn from one another and make supportive connections. They came away from these events with new ideas to improve the efficiency of their departments and lead their teams. They were also inspired by the commitment that other leaders and the business overall made to learning, sharing, and working toward the success.

Company S's approach of providing training on essential topics while also creating space for leaders to build relationship with peers has the dual benefit of instilling useful information *and* strengthening connections. This seems like time well spent.

However, some research has found that leadership training isn't always effective. The finding is that the training doesn't actually lead to improved organizational results because people quickly go back to their old ways of doing things (Beer, Finnström, and Schrader 2016).

I will admit this has been true for me personally. I come home from an inspiring training session, excited by what I've learned, but once I'm back in the office, the routine sets in and I forget the changes I planned on making. Without reminders, reinforcement, and time for habit formation, we tend to go back to old patterns. Does this mean we shouldn't bother to train leaders at all? I don't think that's what it means.

First, leaders need to learn the expected behaviors, policies, and procedures unique to their organization, and simply giving them documentation to read isn't sufficient.

Second, many education programs for professionals don't provide in-depth leadership training, so graduates may not be aware of how to be an effective leader. My accounting studies were extremely light on how to manage people or be an effective mentor. I believe many technical programs are the same.

Yet we expect people with primarily technical educations to lead teams and manage people. Organizations can set up new leaders and their teams for greater success if they provide comprehensive leadership training to employees moving into a leadership role.

Besides, even highly educated leaders or those with great instincts need reminders. And we can always learn from hearing other people's experiences. Topics, such as psychological safety, are also relatively new in executive education, so company-led training provides an opportunity to gain this important knowledge. We should not forsake training but figure out how to get durable results out of it instead.

The benefits of training can be maximized by taking the following steps:

- **Engage the company's top leader to communicate the importance of the sessions.** "Tone from the top" applies here as well. If the top leader of the organization advocates for the benefits of training, it will motivate employees to engage and value the opportunity to learn.
- **Target the training topics to the attendees.** Assess the needs of the leadership team and select topics that will be the most beneficial for the group. If team members are at different skill levels, engage those leaders who are already experts on the topic to present their experiences for their peers to learn from. The experienced leaders will value the ability to help others grow and speaking about their experiences will reinforce the lessons for them as well.
- **Create a psychologically safe environment for the training sessions.** Research has found that training brought greater improvement when groups had already created a psychologically safe environment (Beer, Finnström, and Schrader 2016). If leaders enter the training without fear, are able to focus on the topic at hand, and are willing to share their experiences, the sessions will be more effective and beneficial for all attendees.

- **Reinforce the training when leaders are back in the office.** Methods like in-office refresher classes, sharing newsletters or cases on the training topics, and creating pairs or triads (as discussed in the last section) who keep the topics relevant will assist in keeping the messages from the training sessions top of mind and promote habit formation.

Training also shouldn't be abandoned because it's a critical method to ensure that all leaders are educated on the company's policies around workplace abuse. Research has found that through education on the consequences of abusive conduct, leaders learn that any toxic actions by them will not only damage others but also harm their careers (Priesemuth 2020).

This training may deter abusive actions because the negative impact of the consequences on any potential abusers' career will be clear (Priesemuth 2020). Ideally, we'd prefer leaders who wouldn't harm employees due to their personal values, but failing that, ensuring it's understood that there will be zero tolerance for toxic behavior is a solid second best.

PROVIDE AN ANONYMOUS REPORTING CHANNEL

Unfortunately, despite the use of strong practices in the recruitment, training, and development of leaders, instances of toxic leadership still occur in the work environment. Therefore, staff must have a route to report harmful conduct so action can be taken to correct it.

As discussed in Chapter 6, an HR representative can provide a channel for employees to report toxic behavior. But if an organization doesn't have HR or if someone isn't comfortable sharing with HR, an alternative method to communicate anonymously should be in place.

One option is to create an anonymous email inbox that is controlled by a board of directors or external legal counsel who are authorized to investigate any reported incidents. Providing this channel ensures that employees have a safe route for reporting abusive conduct should an incident occur. It also sets the tone that the company's leaders want to hear about abusive behavior and create a safe work environment. It acts as a negative incentive to leaders who otherwise would allow toxic conduct to persist.

WHY THIS MATTERS TO YOU

Assessing Values Alignment in Leadership Candidates

Values alignment between an organization and its leaders is key in developing a psychologically safe work environment. The interview process should reveal whether potential leaders exhibit the values of the company. The hiring process will be more successful if the hiring manager looks beyond the candidate's résumé by asking the key questions outlined in this chapter.

Provide Leaders with Executive Coaching

Leaders who have been coached have greater emotional awareness. They have improved self-control and higher empathy. If leaders enter coaching with openness to the process, it can support unintentionally toxic leaders to see the impact of their behaviors and take actions to change it.

Engage Meeting Facilitators

Meetings often don't meet their objectives. A skilled facilitator can improve the quality of meeting outcomes while also helping to heal dysfunctional relationships on the team. They are skilled in managing personal dynamics and will work to constructively defuse any tensions or conflicts that arise.

Leadership Team Building

A leadership team is most successful when members truly support the success of one another. Leaders who feel they can go to their peers and safely share their challenges are less likely to become insecure as a result of their difficulties.

Train Leaders

Many education programs don't offer in-depth leadership training, so it's valuable to educate employees on effective leadership skills. Training is also an opportunity to ensure that leaders are aware of conduct that won't be accepted within the organization and the consequences of displaying those behaviors.

Provide an Anonymous Reporting Channel

Employees may not have a trusted person to go to within the company to report the conduct of a toxic leader. This could allow the harmful behavior to continue. An anonymous feedback channel provides a route for staff to report the conduct and sets the tone that the organization takes maintaining a psychologically safe environment seriously.

CHAPTER 13

STRATEGIES TO DEVELOP SECURE LEADER-EMPLOYEE RELATIONSHIPS

"Trust is the glue of life. It's the most essential ingredient in effective communication. It's the foundational principle that holds all relationships."

—Stephen Covey

Healthy leaders are a critical component in building psychologically safe work environments. However, to reap the full benefits of a positive culture, those leaders must actively support employees and build trusting relationships with them.

This chapter will suggest ways that leaders can create healthy, productive relationships with their employees. In such relationships, there is transparency, support, and recognition.

REGULARLY MEET WITH
DIRECT REPORTS

*"Leaders and managers who
invite open dialogue can foster a sense of
'we're all in this together' and avoid creating
a culture where no one speaks up."*

—SHANNON MULLEN O'KEEFE AND JESSICA BUONO

Many leaders use one-to-one meetings and regular check-ins to monitor delegated tasks, but they are also essential tools for developing trusting, secure relationships with employees.

This next story shows some of the benefits of making the time for these meetings.

> Tom, a communication manager at his company, had a very busy leader, Miranda. She was the director of communication in the business and was so busy day to day that Tom rarely got to see her. However, to make up for this, Miranda was committed to having weekly one-to-one meetings, regardless of whether there was something concrete to discuss.
>
> The sessions always involved positive authentic dialogue. Miranda would share progress updates toward business objectives, and Tom would provide the status of his own goals. Then, they'd discuss any challenges he faced. The meetings helped Tom and Miranda build a healthy rapport, and Tom felt informed about the business.
>
> When the company went through a challenging period that involved restructuring and a shift in its strategy, Miranda

maintained her weekly meeting with Tom. This gave him comfort amid a changing environment.

The meetings also benefited Miranda. Tom had an ear to the gossip among the staff. Tom heard a rumor that the company was being bought out, and everyone's jobs were at risk. This rumor was spreading quickly around the organization. He'd even heard that people were going to interviews out of fear they would lose their jobs. Due to their strong relationship, Tom felt comfortable sharing this rumor with Miranda. It was completely untrue; the company wasn't being bought out.

Miranda brought the information to the CEO who held a meeting with all staff to clarify the rumor was untrue. Had Tom not felt comfortable sharing the story with Miranda, the company might have lost valuable employees.

The one-to-one meetings between Tom and Miranda developed their relationship and deepened his commitment to the organization.

Tom isn't alone in his reaction to regular communication with a leader. One study showed that when managers communicated daily with their direct reports, employees were three times more likely to be engaged than when their managers didn't communicate with them regularly (Peart 2019). Miranda and Tom may not have communicated daily, but the reliability of their sessions still significantly increased Tom's commitment to the organization and made him feel valued.

Benefits to Regular Meetings
with Direct Reports

The employee will be more comfortable sharing mistakes and personal challenges.

If a leader and employee successfully build a healthy, productive relationship, the employee will know that any personal information shared with their boss won't be used against them. As a result, the leader will have the opportunity to provide help when needed and support the employee to learn from their experiences.

I've seen the benefit of this firsthand. One of my employees was facing considerable challenges with a night school course. They had misjudged the workload and were having a hard time juggling the combined demands of their job and the course.

They shared the problem with me, knowing that I wouldn't blame them for the misjudgment but instead would support them. We reduced their workload for the remainder of the class. This way, they met the school commitments without worrying about meeting work commitments at the same time. The alternative would have been either failure at school or poor performance at work.

Due to our open, honest working relationship, neither occurred. The employee did well in the course and continued to be a reliable, committed worker.

Employees will be more likely to share information they've heard about the business.

Through ongoing direct communication with staff, leaders can establish they will not react negatively when difficult or unexpected news is shared with them. As a result, employees will be more comfortable sharing such information. Leaders will have greater awareness of what's happening at all levels of the company and will have the opportunity to resolve issues before they become bigger problems.

The story illustrated this when Tom shared the buy-out rumor with Miranda. Miranda might not otherwise have learned about the acquisition gossip upsetting the company's staff.

Leaders can ensure communication efforts are reaching employees as intended.

Direct discussions with staff are opportunities to check whether corporate communications have effectively explained situations or pending changes. Information often gets lost in translation or convoluted during conversation among peers; although leaders may think the communication was clear, what the employees actually hear can be very different, depending on their focus and bias.

In an Edelman (2019) survey, employees said that their top source of information about their companies was informal conversation with coworkers. A message can easily become distorted when coworkers discuss it with each other and introduce their biases. One-to-one meetings between leaders and employees can clear up any inaccuracies or points of confusion.

Tips for Successful One-to-One Meetings

Face-to-face is best.

I advise against one-to-ones over the phone unless it's the only option. I've found that too much is lost in the communication with my employees if they can't see my face to get a true understanding of my intent.

If information about impending changes or constructive feedback is being shared, it's critical for the employee to see their leader's expression. If their leader is calm about a change, the employee will be too, and feedback lands better if the employee sees on their boss's face that they're providing the feedback to help the employee succeed.

The leader should be open.

Leaders who are open and honest about who they are and show some vulnerability will build greater trust with their employees.

If I'm having a difficult day, I don't shy away from letting my team know this. I'm human, too. Some days, I haven't slept well, am dealing with a personal difficulty, or am finding a work task hard to get through. Being honest that some days are challenging for me opens up space for employees to share when they're having difficulties.

However, I establish a balance by sharing enough to be open while still being positive about my ability, and my team's ability, to achieve success and overcome challenges. Disclosure about our challenges shouldn't undermine confidence in us or the company.

Avoid canceling.

If one-to-one meetings are frequently canceled, it sends a signal to the employee that the meetings aren't important. Even if there isn't a lot to discuss, it's essential to have the check-in. The meeting may not take the full time allotted, but something may be going on that the leader wasn't aware of that comes out during the meeting. We want our staff to be reliable, so we should be, too.

SUPPORT EMPLOYEES TO FIND THEIR TALENTS AND REACH THEIR PERSONAL GOALS

Part of our roles as leaders is to identify talent and support employees to grow professionally and personally. In doing so, we're helping the company by ensuring that talent within the organization is maximized while also helping people grow their careers and be prepared for promotions. This is a win-win that benefits both the employee and the business.

Supporting staff development also creates a strong corporate culture within which people feel they can reach their full potential. Organizations that actively support their employees' growth will benefit from a secure, productive workforce, longer tenures, and improved succession planning.

However, identifying talent isn't a simple task. I've found it's not always evident what aptitudes our employees have. And many people are insecure and don't realize their own talent. They may not have been in situations that allowed their skills to shine through.

I joined a company as the head of finance and was introduced to my team. One of the women on my team quietly hung back. She was the Accounts Receivable (AR) clerk. She was nervous and very formal when she came for our first one-to-one meeting.

Yet, I could tell she was smart and had a lot of potential. I learned she'd been about to leave the company but had decided to stay when she found out that a new leader was coming on board. The person whom I replaced hadn't given her any opportunity and had instilled insecurity with his bullying. I observed her work for the next month and saw she was capable of more than her position was asking of her.

I changed her title to AR specialist and supported her to go to credit management school. Through the more senior title and my support, her confidence began to grow, and her insecurity diminished.

The business expanded. Within a year, we added to the AR team and I promoted her to AR manager. She went on to complete her credit manager certificate and eventually moved on to a credit manager position in a much larger organization. All that she had needed was someone to see her talent and believe in her. I feel extremely fortunate I had the pleasure of being that person.

Determining what an employee is capable of, what they want, and how we can support them to achieve their goals requires ongoing conversations about their objectives and their performance. It also requires observation of their work. We may see opportunities and talents that our employee doesn't see. We may also see challenges in their skillset that they don't. Both topics should be addressed. And the leader should support the employee in their efforts to overcome any challenges and maximize the opportunities available to them.

This honest dialogue will build a safe, trusting relationship, reduce insecurity, and increase the likelihood the employee will grow within the company, and the business will benefit from their full potential.

Although it's ideal when employees grow within our teams, their aspirations may or may not include a long future with our organization. The reality is that most employees will eventually move on, and an open conversation about this will be better for all involved.

Discussions with an employee about their professional goals and growth shouldn't focus solely on their potential with their current employer. If we are truly supporting our staff, we are looking at the whole person, not just the part of the person that can benefit our organization. Janice did exactly that in this next story.

> Kacy, one of the junior marketing analysts on Janice's team, was performing well in her role but didn't seem engaged. In their next one-to-one, Janice asked Kacy how she was feeling about her work and where she saw her career going. Kacy had been at the company for two years, and during that time, they'd built an honest relationship, so Kacy was comfortable opening up to Janice. She told Janice that her dream had always been to become a chef.
>
> As it turned out, Kacy had an opportunity to take a part-time job as an apprentice chef on the weekends. Janice encouraged her to take the job to get a sense of whether it was the right career for her. Kacy accepted the weekend position.
>
> Janice hadn't expected any issues with Kacy's performance because of the side job. But she certainly hadn't expected the marked improvement in Kacy's engagement at work either. This was the product of Kacy's appreciation for Janice's support to pursue her dream without having to hide it.

Kacy stayed in her position at the company for two more years while she trained to be a chef. During that time, Janice benefited from the excellent performance of a committed, efficient junior analyst. It can be quite difficult to keep employees in junior positions for long because they often want to progress and obtain promotions. It was excellent for Janice's team to have a stable, productive person in the role, even though it wasn't her long-term plan.

If we develop honest relationships with our staff, it will increase their engagement for the time they are with the company because they can be transparent. They will also be advocates for the organization after they leave. This will help the business's reputation and future recruitment efforts. The company will also have time to prepare for the employee's departure rather than planning for a future with the employee, only to be surprised by two weeks' notice at some inopportune time.

RECOGNIZE EMPLOYEES' EFFORTS

"The deepest desire of the human spirit
is to be acknowledged."

—Stephen Covey

Recognition holds a place on the Maslow's hierarchy of needs for a good reason; to be genuinely happy, humans need to feel valued.

Most people get some fulfillment from the satisfaction of a job well done, but that sense of satisfaction is maximized when someone else, especially someone we respect, recognizes our effort and our work. Sadly, a survey of employed Americans revealed that 82 percent of survey respondents didn't feel that their supervisors recognized them enough for their contributions (Novak 2016). Our staff perform tasks every day, and we likely appreciate them every day. There is a risk, however, that we get used to the performance and don't officially recognize it as much as we should.

The survey noted above also found that 40 percent of employed Americans say they'd put more energy into their work if they were recognized more often (Novak 2016). Research also found that experiencing gratitude from their manager can make employees more productive (Grant and Gino 2010). Through greater recognition, an organization will benefit from a more secure workforce and a harder working one.

For many, the benefits yielded by recognition are taken to an even higher level if it's given publicly. Natalia Peart (2019) in her *Harvard Business Review* article "Making Work Less Stressful and More Engaging for Your Employees" reported that "publicly recognizing the hard work and contributions of team members decreases feelings of stress and increases feelings of connection and belonging. Research has shown that companies with high-recognition cultures perform better and have less turnover than those that don't."

However, even a simple thank-you, which costs the company nothing, can go a long way to increase employee satisfaction. I will add, however, the recognition needs to be authentic and specific (Gibson, O'Leary, and Weintraub 2020); people will sense if gratitude is just window dressing, and it won't have the same effect.

For your consideration, here is an overview of recognition programs that I have seen work well in organizations:

- **Peer-to-Peer Recognition.** Create a program for peers to acknowledge one another's contributions. This can be manual or automated. Online platforms are available where staff can submit a recognition message and even allocate dollars from a monthly budget to award their peers. Typically, these awards are first reviewed and approved by HR. Alternatively, a low-tech option is to designate a recognition wall where employees can post sticky-note messages of thanks to their peers.
- **Monthly or Quarterly Recognition Awards.** Periodic rewards are an effective way to honor exceptional

performance and recognize highly valued behaviors. The awards can be announced at all-hands meetings to provide an element of public recognition. The person may be selected directly by leadership or through the peer-to-peer awards, or both. The reason for the recognition should be shared so that conduct that aligns with the company's values is modeled.

- **Annual Awards.** Annual awards can be given to employees who consistently live the values of the organization for that calendar year while performing optimally in their role. This could be a peer-voted award and a leader-voted award. Again, this sets a tone for the behavior the company values.

You may choose to do some, none, or all of the recognition programs shared here, but finding a method that works for your business and for your staff will reap countless returns. The exact method used to give recognition isn't important as long as the result is that employees feel valued and are recognized when they've done a great job.

ADAPTING LEADERSHIP STYLE TO EMPLOYEE NEEDS

Often, leaders will have employees who are at different stages in their career life cycle. This requires leaders to adapt their style to the needs of each person. Making such adjustments ensures that those who need support receive it and those who don't aren't over-managed. Glen applied this flexible approach well in this next story.

Glen's team of four was responsible for purchasing at Company X. Two employees had been in their positions for many years and two had been hired within the past twelve months. Glen believed in leading with trust. He gave his team the autonomy to get their work done as they saw fit and within a schedule that worked for them, as long as they met their deadlines.

However, one of Glen's newer hires, Madelyn, was struggling with the complexity of the company's purchasing needs. Glen recognized that he had to shift his leadership style to accommodate Madelyn's needs. He spoke to her to determine how he could support her.

Madelyn was having a hard time prioritizing her work amid the multitude of departmental requests. Glen suggested they meet every morning for five minutes to review the needs of the day and develop a plan for her. They did this for four weeks.

In the sessions, they reviewed the requirements of the day and Glen shared tips on prioritization and time management. By the end of the four weeks, Madelyn was taking the lead in their meetings. The skills that Glen had taught Madelyn had become second nature. With his support, she'd gained the confidence to face the complexity of her role with calmness, rather than becoming overwhelmed by the volume of work.

If an employee is new to the team, having performance challenges, going through a difficult personal time, or learning something new, they may have a high need for the leader's time and attention. On the other hand, if someone has been at the company for several years, is performing in a role they know well, and isn't experiencing any personal challenges, their need for their leader's time should be low.

The leadership skill is to thoughtfully assess how each team member is doing and provide them with the appropriate type and amount of management attention. The leader should share their understanding of each person's situation with them and explain the approach they plan to take. The goal is for the employee to agree that the approach is suitable for their developmental level and will in fact help them resolve any problems.

If they don't agree, it creates an opportunity for discussion exploring how the leader and employee see the details of the situation differently and where their expectations don't align. Only good things can come from an open discussion like that.

Glen's communication with Madelyn was skillful and attentive to her feelings. He realized that she needed a different level of support than the rest of his team, so approached her, without creating a threat, to figure out how to adjust his style to support her.

I will note that although typically micromanagement is a cause of insecurity, there may be times when it's needed and even welcomed by employees. Glen's daily meetings with Madelyn to review her work could be considered micromanagement, but the intention is support rather than watching over her. Sometimes people need support and training to ensure they succeed in their roles. Micromanaging can be used successfully if the employee is aware there will be a high level of management for a period of time, and they understand it's to support their success rather than to dominate them.

Meeting Regularly with Direct Reports

One-to-one meetings with direct reports are fundamental to the development of trusting, secure working relationships. They are ideal for building rapport, sharing information, and unearthing possible future issues. With that relationship in place, employees will be more comfortable discussing personal and professional challenges that could be impacting their performance.

Support Employees to Find Their Talents and Reach Their Personal Goals

Supporting an employee's future contributes to a strong business, as staff feel empowered to reach their full potential and maximize their contribution to the company's success. Employees will feel secure in an environment that supports their growth and with leaders who care about their future.

Recognize Employees' Efforts

Feeling valued and recognized is a distinct human need. If employees feel recognized, they are likely to work harder and be more productive. Recognition will also confirm for the employee when they are doing a great job and help calm any insecure feelings.

Adapting Our Leadership Style to the Needs of Employees

By assessing each employee's needs, leaders can provide support to those who need it and create safety in their role and not over-manage those who don't need as much oversight.

CHAPTER 14

IS THIS ALL TOO MUCH? CAN'T PEOPLE JUST DO THEIR JOBS?

Some readers will wonder if everything I've gone through in this book is all "too much." You may be asking yourself, "Won't this kind of coddling only lead to bad behavior and taking advantage?"

I understand that view, as we've all seen situations where people take advantage of a kind gesture or milk a situation for all it's worth. However, I believe that when we see this occur, it's because the perpetrator isn't operating from a psychologically secure place. Their needs haven't been met, and what we may see as taking advantage is actually the person trying to get those needs met or to protect themselves.

Alternatively, they believe they've been mistreated in the situation, so they feel entitled to take what they can from it. If we can create a workplace that's psychologically safe and minimizes activation of the defense mechanisms, less "taking advantage" and more working together toward common goals will occur.

I believe that most of us are good. Most of us want to do well and don't want to let each other down. When we act in ways that go against this, it's usually out of self-preservation. It's up to leaders to create environments where self-preservation isn't the sole driver for all of our decisions.

We need to create workplaces where we're all looking out for each other because we understand the success of others leads to our own success. We need work environments where employees can safely be themselves and understand the value they bring to the company. Doing this will allow people to come out of their shells, like I did, and achieve more than they or anyone imagined they could. Doing so will lead to achievements for all: the employee, the business, and the customer.

An employee who doesn't feel safe in their company or their role will not be motivated or capable of pushing for the success of the business. The quantity of the work they complete will be reduced and the quality will suffer. Consider the missed deadlines and opportunities and the disappointment of customers when expectations aren't met.

In a healthy work environment, employees will reach their full potential, maximize the quality and quantity of their work, and inspire each other to reach higher. In a psychologically safe workplace, staff have the mental space to focus on their objectives, and great things can be achieved.

The downsides of not taking the actions outlined in this book to create a safe work environment are far greater than the risk of some people taking advantage. A healthy culture will attract great people, while a toxic unsafe one will attract no one and scare away the high performers who may unknowingly end up there.

Having said this, I will not deny that jobs exist where leaders can get what they need from employees without much consideration for the culture and the environment. However, these aren't jobs that require long-term commitments, innovative ideas, collaboration among peers, and excellent customer service.

I've worked in companies where everyone was focused on increasing the stock price and exiting with a lot of money in their pockets without any consideration of culture. This can work if the big payout happens quickly and everyone moves on to their next projects. But if it doesn't happen quickly and people stew and stay within the nonculture for long, negative impacts will come to light. People's patience with bad behavior diminishes and companies will lose employees whom they may have hoped would stick around.

A company may also get away with not dealing with cultural issues if the business is process-oriented and requires no innovation. This type of workplace will attract people who just want to do a day's work and get out. This can work for some time. However, eventually a lack of innovation and novel ideas will allow the business to be surpassed by competitors in a normal market.

With all the information shared in this book, you can now assess the type of workplace you have. You can evaluate the goals and structure of your business and determine whether the current state of your culture is impacting the achievement of your goals.

You now recognize that for innovation and maximum productivity, businesses need to create open, transparent, psychologically safe work environments into which people can bring their whole selves. You understand the negative effect on performance when employees only show the part of who they are they think will be accepted and hide their weaknesses. You see the need for all of us to open our minds and understand one another, instead of reacting and letting our protective instincts drive short-term actions without any thought to long-term repercussions. This openness and understanding allows us to build healthier work relationships and environments and leads to greater business success.

This isn't a purely ethical argument. If a company needs innovation, long-tenured employees, collaboration, and excellent customer service but doesn't have a healthy work environment, the business is not achieving its full potential.

For the success of your business, you need to assess your organization and determine which of the recommendations from this book will improve the culture and engage staff in the creation of a safe healthy workplace.

I think all of us also need to look at our companies from an ethical, humanistic perspective and assess how the current culture is impacting our employees.

Do you want to have an environment that causes psychological harm to people, even if you need them employed for only a season or a project? Do you want to have an environment that allows a bully to cause such psychological damage to someone that it stays with them for the rest of their lives? I think the answer to this for most of us is a resounding no. We can do the right thing for people *and* the right thing for business.

My challenge to you is to think about the elements in this book that had an impact on you. Think about the memories that were triggered. It's hard to face that the behaviors that were caused by our own insecurities may have created insecurities in others. But we can heal, and we can make up for past conduct by being better leaders today.

We can spend more time now trying to understand what's happening with others. If someone is insecure, ask why. If you're in a position to do so, advocate for others as much as you would yourself. In the long term, this will improve your life as much as it improves theirs, and the positive impact on your company will be profound.

A secure workforce will enable the success of a business through their loyalty, ability to innovate and grow, and the high levels of productivity that result when we can truly focus on our work.

REFERENCES

2019 Edelman Trust Barometer. Edelman, January 20, 2019. https://www.edelman.com/trust/2019-trust-barometer.

Bariso, Justin. "Google Has an Official Process in Place for Learning from Failure—and It's Absolutely Brilliant." *Inc.*, May 14, 2018. https://www.inc.com/justin-bariso/meet-postmortem-googles-brilliant-process-tool-for-learning-from-failure.html.

Baumeister, Roy F., Ellen Bratslavsky, Catrin Finkenauer, and Kathleen D. Vohs. "Bad Is Stronger than Good." *Review of General Psychology* 5, no. 4 (December 2001): 323–370. https://doi.org/10.1037/1089-2680.5.4.323.

Beer, Michael, Magnus Finnström, and Derek Schrader. "Why Leadership Training Fails—and What to Do about It." *Harvard Business Review*, October 2016. https://hbr.org/2016/10/why-leadership-training-fails-and-what-to-do-about-it.

Blount, Sally, and Paul Leinwand. "Why Are We Here?" *Harvard Business Review*, November–December 2019. https://hbr.org/2019/11/why-are-we-here.

Blount, Sally, and Shana Carroll. "Overcome Resistance to Change with Two Conversations." *Harvard Business Review*, May 16, 2017. https://hbr.org/2017/05/overcome-resistance-to-change-with-two-conversations.

Bortz, Daniel. "What Can I Do about Workplace Bullying?" Monster. Accessed May 26, 2021. https://www.monster.com/career-advice/article/workplace-bullying-what-can-you-do.

Brim, Brian J. "Strength-Based Leadership: Building Stability in Followers." Gallup. March 24, 2016. https://www.gallup.com/cliftonstrengths/en/250817/strengths-based-leadership-building-stability-followers.aspx.

Brown, Scott, and Jennifer Robison. "How to Communicate to Create Stability Despite Uncertainty." Gallup. May 21, 2020. https://www.gallup.com/workplace/311 288/communicate-create-stability-despite-uncertainty.aspx.

Carter, Christine. "Seven Ways to Cope with Uncertainty: What Should We Do When Everything Feels So Out of Control?" *Greater Good Magazine*, July 27, 2020. https://greatergood.berkeley.edu/article/item/seven_ways_to_cope_with _uncertainty.

Carucci, Ron. "How to Deal with a Passive-Aggressive Boss." *Harvard Business Review*, January 24, 2018. https://hbr.org/2018/01/how-to-deal-with-a -passive-aggressive-boss.

Cascio, Wayne F. "Costing Human Resources." Human Resource Management 5, (January 2015). https://doi.org/10.1002/9781118785317.weom050012.

Chamorro-Premuzic, Tomas. "How and Why We Lie at Work." *Harvard Business Review*, January 2, 2015. https://hbr.org/2015/01/how-and-why-we-lie-at-work.

Cherry, Kendra. "The 5 Levels of Maslow's Hierarchy of Needs." Verywell Mind. Accessed February 19, 2021. https://www.verywellmind.com/what-is -maslows-hierarchy-of-needs-4136760.

Cherry, Kendra. "What Is the Negativity Bias?" Verywell Mind. Accessed February 19, 2020. https://www.verywellmind.com/negative-bias-4589618.

Chesnut, Robert. "How to Build a Company That (Actually) Values Integrity." *Harvard Business Review*, July 30, 2020. https://hbr.org/2020/07/how-to-build -a-company-that-actually-values-integrity.

Conner, Cheryl. "Overcoming the Biggest Challenge in Business: Your Own Insecurity." *Forbes*, May 4, 2013. https://www.forbes.com/sites/cherylsnappconner /2013/05/04/overcoming-the-biggest-challenge-in-business-your-own-inse curity/?sh=623fd60e3aa4.

Covey, Stephen R., A. Roger Merrill, and Rebecca R. Merrill. *First Things First*. New York: Simon & Schuster, 1994.

Cuncic, Arlin. "Amygdala Hijack and the Fight or Flight Response." Verywell Mind. Accessed February 19, 2021. https://www.verywellmind.com/what-happens -during-an-amygdala-hijack-4165944.

Dalio, Ray. *Principles*. New York: Simon & Schuster, 2017.

Dekker, Sidney W. A., and Wilmar B. Schaufeli. "The Effects of Job Insecurity on Psychological Health and Withdrawal: A Longitudinal Study." *Australian Psychologist* 30, no. 1 (1995): 57–63. https://doi.org/10.1080/00050069508259607.

DePaul, Kristi. "How to Find Out if a Company's Culture Is Right for You." *Harvard Business Review*, November 30, 2020. https://hbr.org/2020/11/how-to-find-out-if-a-companys-culture-is-right-for-you.

Drucker, Peter F. *Managing Oneself*. Boston: Harvard Business Press, 2008.

Edmondson, Amy C. "Strategies for Learning from Failure." *Harvard Business Review*, April 2011. https://hbr.org/2011/04/strategies-for-learning-from-failure.

Edmondson, Amy C. *The Fearless Organization: Creating Psychological Safety in the Workplace for Learning, Innovation, and Growth*. Hoboken, NJ: Wiley, 2018.

Gibson, Kerry Roberts, Kate O'Leary, and Joseph R. Weintraub. "The Little Things That Make Employees Feel Appreciated." *Harvard Business Review*, January 23, 2020. https://hbr.org/2020/01/the-little-things-that-make-employees-feel-appreciated.

Goleman, Daniel. *Emotional Intelligence: Why It Can Matter More than IQ*. New York: Bantam Books, 1995.

Grant, Adam M. (@AdamMGrant). 2018. "If you think you have to be an asshole…" Twitter, August 3, 2018. https://twitter.com/adammgrant/status/1025355025399402496?lang=en.

Grant, Adam M. (@AdamMGrant). 2020. "Dear leaders: Do everything you can to avoid layoffs…" Twitter, May 13, 2020. https://twitter.com/AdamMGrant/status/1260554840457043969?s=20.

Grant, Adam M. (@AdamMGrant). 2020. "In every team and every organization…" Twitter, August 3, 2020. https://twitter.com/adammgrant/status/1290260434537201664?lang=en.

Grant, Adam M. (@AdamMGrant). 2020. "You don't procrastinate to avoid work…" Twitter, March 10, 2020. https://twitter.com/AdamMGrant/status/1237347993776504837?s=20.

Grant, Adam M., and Francesca Gino. "A Little Thanks Goes a Long Way: Explaining Why Gratitude Expressions Motivate Prosocial Behavior." *Journal of Personality and Social Psychology* 98, no. 6 (2010): 946–955. https://doi.org/10.1037/a0017935.

Greenberg, Melanie. "The Top 3 Reasons Why You Self-Sabotage and How to Stop: Faulty Thinking and Fear of Failure Play a Part." *Psychology Today*, June 11, 2018. https://www.psychologytoday.com/us/blog/the-mindful-self-express/201806/the-top-3-reasons-why-you-self-sabotage-and-how-stop.

Guo, Liang, Stijn Decoster, Mayowa T. Babalola, Leander De Shutter, Omale A. Garba, and Katrin Riisla. "Authoritarian Leadership and Employee Creativity: The Moderating Role of Psychological Capital and the Mediating Role of Fear and Defensive Silence." *Journal of Business Research* 92, (November 2018): 219–230. https://doi.org/10.1016/j.jbusres.2018.07.034.

Hurt, Karin, and David Dye. "The Main Reasons Employees Don't Speak Their Mind at Work." *Fast Company*, July 13, 2020. https://www.fastcompany.com/90526638/the-main-reasons-employees-dont-speak-their-mind-at-work.

Kusy, Mitchell, and Elizabeth Holloway. *Toxic Workplace!: Managing Toxic Personalities and Their Systems of Power.* San Francisco: Jossey-Bass, 2009.

McClean, Shawn, Stephen H. Courtright, Troy A. Smith, and Junhyok Yim. "Stop Making Excuses for Toxic Bosses." *Harvard Business Review*, January 19, 2021. https://hbr.org/2021/01/stop-making-excuses-for-toxic-bosses.

McKeown, Greg. "The Emotional Boundaries You Need at Work." *Harvard Business Review*, July 24, 2014. https://hbr.org/2014/07/the-emotional-boundaries-you-need-at-work.

Menon, Tanya, and Leigh Thompson. "Envy at Work." *Harvard Business Review*, April 2010. https://hbr.org/2010/04/envy-at-work.

Messenböck, Reinhard, Markus Klevenz, Anja Marzuillo, and Mike Galicija. "Implementing HR Excellence: Four Levers to Improve Human Resources Performance." Boston Consulting Group. July 15, 2015. https://www.bcg.com/en-gr/publications/2015/people-organization-implementing-hr-excellence-four-levers-improve-human-resources-performance.

Michigan State University. "How Incivility Spreads in the Workplace." *Science-Daily*, August 10, 2016. https://www.sciencedaily.com/releases/2016/08/160810104409.htm.

Novak, David. "Recognizing Employees Is the Simplest Way to Improve Morale." *Harvard Business Review*, May 9, 2016. https://hbr.org/2016/05/recognizing-employees-is-the-simplest-way-to-improve-morale.html.

O'Keefe, Shannon Mullen, and Jessica Buono. "Crisis Communication: How Great Leaders Stop Rumors before They Start." Gallup. April 3, 2020. https://www.gallup.com/workplace/297545/crisis-communication-great-leaders-stop-rumors-start.aspx.

Peart, Natalia. "Making Work Less Stressful and More Engaging for Your Employees." *Harvard Business Review*, November 5, 2019. https://hbr.org/2019/11/making-work-less-stressful-and-more-engaging-for-your-employees.

Porath, Christine. "How Rudeness Stops People from Working Together." *Harvard Business Review*, January 20, 2017. https://hbr.org/2017/01/how-rudeness-stops-people-from-working-together.

Priesemuth, Manuela. "Time's Up for Toxic Workplaces." *Harvard Business Review*, June 19, 2020. https://hbr.org/2020/06/times-up-for-toxic-workplaces.

Robinson, Bryan. "New Study Says Workplace Bullying on Rise: What You Can Do during National Bullying Prevention Month." *Forbes*, October 11, 2019. https://www.forbes.com/sites/bryanrobinson/2019/10/11/new-study-says-workplace-bullying-on-rise-what-can-you-do-during-national-bullying-prevention-month/?sh=542e99972a0d.

Robison, Jennifer. "What Followers Want from Leaders: A Q&A with Tom Rath and Barry Conchie, Authors of *Strengths Based Leadership*." Gallup. January 8, 2009. https://news.gallup.com/businessjournal/113542/What-Followers-Want-From-Leaders.aspx.

Rock, David. "Managing with the Brain in Mind." Oxford Leadership. 2016. http://www.oxfordleadership.com/wp-content/uploads/2016/08/oxford-leadership-article-managing-with-brain-in-mind.pdf.

Salovey, Peter, and Judith Rodin. "Some Antecedents and Consequences of Social-Comparison Jealousy." *Journal of Personality and Social Psychology* 47, no. 4 (1984): 780–792. https://doi.org/10.1037/0022-3514.47.4.780.

Sarason, Irwin G., Barbara R. Sarason, and Gregory R. Pierce. "Cognitive Interference." In *International Handbook of Personality and Intelligence*, edited by Donald H. Saklofske and Moshe Zeidner, 285–296. New York: Springer, 1995. https://doi.org/10.1007/978-1-4757-5571-8_14.

Schieman, Scott. "Feeling Underpaid? There Are Health Consequences to That." *The Globe and Mail*, March 19, 2015. https://www.theglobeandmail.com/life/health-and-fitness/health-advisor/feeling-underpaid-there-are-health-consequences-to-that/article23541907/.

Sirois, Fuschia, and Timothy Pychyl. "Procrastination and the Priority of Short-Term Mood Regulation: Consequences for Future Self." *Social and Personality Psychology Compass* 7, no. 2 (February 2013): 115–27. https://doi.org/doi:10.1111/spc3.12011.

Smith, Christie, and Kenji Yoshino. "Uncovering Talent: A New Model of Inclusion." Deloitte. 2019. www2.deloitte.com/content/dam/Deloitte/us/Documents/about-deloitte/us-about-deloitte-uncovering-talent-a-new-model-of-inclusion.pdf.

State of the American Workplace Report. Gallup, 2017. https://www.gallup.com
/workplace/285818/state-american-workplace-report.aspx.

Tepper, Bennet J. "Consequences of Abusive Supervision." *The Academy of Management Journal* 43, no. 2 (April 2000): 178–90. https://doi.org/10.5465/1556375.

The John Maxwell Company. "Insecurity: An Explosive Quality in the Life of a Leader." John C. Maxwell. July 7, 2014. https://www.johnmaxwell.com/blog
/insecurity-an-explosive-quality-in-the-life-of-a-leader/.

Wahba, Mahmoud A., and Lawrence G. Bridwell. "Maslow Reconsidered: A Review of Research on the Need Hierarchy Theory." *Organizational Behavior and Human Performance* 15, no. 2 (April 1976): 212–240. https://doi.org/10
.1016/0030-5073(76)90038-6.

Weber, Svenja, and Gianpiero Petriglieri. "To Overcome Your Insecurity, Recognize Where It Really Comes From." *Harvard Business Review*, June 27, 2018.
https://hbr.org/2018/06/to-overcome-your-insecurity-recognize-where-it-really
-comes-from?autocomplete=true.

Zappos. "Zappos 10 Core Values." Zappos Insights. Accessed May 26, 2021. https:
//www.zapposinsights.com/about/core-values.

Made in the USA
Middletown, DE
12 July 2024

57232123R00177